Gethsemane to Calvary

by
Olin S. Reigstad

Published by Augsburg Publishing House · Minneapolis

Manufactured in the United States of America
Printed by Augsburg Publishing House, Minneapolis 15, Minnesota

Contents

iii

A Lonely Vigil

Then was Jesus led up of the spirit into the wilderness to be tempted of the devil. And when he had fasted forty nights, he was afterward an hungred. And when the tempter came to him, he said, If thou be the Son of God, command that these stones be made bread. But he answered and said, It is written, Man shall not live by bread alone, but by every word that proceedeth out of the mouth of God. Then the devil taketh him up into the holy city, and setteth him on a pinnacle of the temple, and saith unto him, If thou be the Son of God, cast thyself down: for it is written, He shall give his angels charge concerning thee: and in their hands they shall bear thee up, lest at any time thou dash thy foot against a stone. Jesus said unto him, It is written again, Thou shalt not tempt the Lord thy God. Again, the devil taketh him up into an exceeding high mountain, and sheweth him all the kingdoms of the world, and the glory of them; and saith unto him, All these things will I give thee, if thou wilt fall down and worship me. Then saith Jesus unto him, Get thee hence, Satan: for it is written, Thou shalt worship the Lord thy God, and him only shalt thou serve. Then the devil leaveth him, and, behold, angels came and ministered unto him. Matthew 4:1-11

THE story of Christ's temptation, the lonely vigil in the wilderness, must have been detailed by the Lord Himself. The mysterious experiences of those forty days were not observed by human eyes. Mark says that our Lord was "in the wilderness alone." The angels of God must have watched from above with abhorrence and apprehension, but the angels did not write the Gospels.

The temptation comes as a counterpart of the baptism which ended with the declaration of the divine Sonship of Jesus. It was the next necessary step in the process of fulfilling all righteousness. Jesus met the repeated attacks of Satan on the same footing as other men. Thereby He acquired an experimental acquaintance with the force of our temptations. His desire may have been a more undisturbed communion with the Father and an unbroken contemplation of the work before Him. What He anticipated as a calm and hallowed intercourse with heaven was instead a time of dire conflict. Hell's subtlety was set to overwhelm Him and to destroy salvation before it could bud and flower.

For forty days and nights He was alone, and Mark and Luke both inform us that during the whole time He was tempted of the devil. But it is not until the end of this time that we are permitted to see the forms which His temptations

assumed. Mark says "he was with the wild beasts."
Perhaps the devil sought to destroy the Savior's
firmness by terror. We have reason to assume that
since He was human, He was exhausted by the
long abstinence and was grievously hungry. Every
circumstance conspired to make the allurement of
food as strong as possible. Did He look like the
Son of God then?

Satan came to Him and said, "If thou be the
Son of God, command that these stones be made
bread." You can neutralize your hunger and the
curse if you are the Son of God. The food that the
wilderness refuses to give can be taken by force.
Your arbitrary exercise of divine power will make
even the wilderness yield food. Make bread, eat
bread and be comfortable in the wilderness. That
was Satan's logic. But Jesus seizes upon a word of
God which is to the point and apropos: "Man does
not live by bread alone." God could sustain Him,
even there, in a thousand ways. If God wanted
Him to eat, could He not again, as in the wilderness, provide manna for Jesus, as He then had
provided manna for the hosts of Israel? The logic
Jesus exercises is this, that He must not employ
miraculous powers to provide food, for that would
be to distrust God. Nor will He provide bread for
Himself in a way not open to His brethren. He
became a man "so that he might in all things be
tried as we are."

But Satan is not satisfied. He directs the shafts of his temptation at the very heart of Jesus when he shows Him all the kingdoms of the world and with Satanic assurance tells the Son of God that He can have all these kingdoms, all their glory, all their wealth, all their people, everything that eye can behold—"if thou wilt fall down and worship me." Satan calculated to make quick work of it, but Jesus had an answer again: "For it is written, Thou shalt worship the Lord thy God, and him only shalt thou serve." Be gone! "Get thee behind me, Satan," and the arch enemy, the deceiver, the destroyer of all that is good, slunk into the darkness from which he came, and the angels, the messengers of God, came down from heaven and ministered to Jesus and He was fed by bread which cometh down out of heaven.

The "why" of this lonely vigil is answered in the Book of Hebrews by these heaven-inspired words of a holy writer: "For we have not an high priest who can not be touched by the feeling of our infirmities, but was in all points tempted like as we are, yet without sin." That is a good answer. If He is going to help me, He must learn by experience the bitter assaults to which I am subject. He must face the same temptations that come to me and yet not yield.

Just as Satan, by his paradisiacal victory over Adam, had placed men in bondage and carried

the sons of God captive, so must Jesus, the second
Adam, here in the wilderness wrest from the hand
of Satan the spoils of that first temptation. Paul
says, "For as in Adam all die, even so in Christ
shall all be made alive." "As through the disobe-
dience of one, many became sinners so through the
obedience of one shall many be made righteous."
And further in the Book of Hebrews we read:
"Wherefore in all things it behooved him to be
made like unto his brethren, that he might be a
merciful and faithful high priest. For in that he
himself hath suffered being tempted he is able to
succor them that are tempted." Those answers to
the wilderness experience of Jesus are logical and
filled with comfort and assurance for those that are
troubled and tempted.

For Christians there will always be temptations
to thwart the will of God. The child of the world
escapes because he is already determined to destroy
the will of God. When such a one avoids doing
evil, it is not because he has yielded to the will
of God; rather, he refrains because that is expe-
dient for him. Not all Christians have the same
weakness, but all have some weakness. That is
where the attack will occur. No time ever comes
in the life of the Christian when he is above
temptation. That is why the Word of God cau-
tions, "Wherefore let him that thinketh he stand-
eth take heed lest he fall." That is a good warning

against the universality, the subtlety and the malignancy of temptation. Woe to the Christian who relaxes his vigilance and is forced to say, "I fell into sin because I deemed myself beyond temptation."

There is a moral value to be gleaned out of temptations where, by the grace of God, we have vanquished the tempter. We can hardly think of moral strength and character without it. "Talent may be found in solitude, but character is formed in the storms of life." Jesus, who knew the power of temptation so well, said, "Watch and pray, lest ye enter into temptation." Let no one ever say, "I am sure of myself." The unexpected may happen in a moment. We must discipline ourselves by watchful prayer, and even then the struggle may be terrific. No fall is impossible or unthinkable. Moses was a good man, meek and humble, but anger overcame him and he was excluded from the joys of recaptured Canaan. David had a deep, abiding and reverent respect for God and all that was good, he was a man after God's own heart; yet lust engulfed him and he became a murderer, too. And Peter, who loved Jesus so much and wanted to do so much for Him, fell into a disgraceful sin of denial before the pointed finger of a servant girl.

Temptations can be met. St. Paul says, "There hath no temptation taken you but such as is common to man: but God is faithful, who will not suffer you to be tempted above that ye are able; but will with the temptation also make a way to escape, that ye may be able to bear it." If some have failed because of presumption, we must not fail because of discouragement. No one is tempted beyond the power of resistance. People sometimes say, "The temptation was too much for me, it was too strong." That is only an alibi. The Christian says with Paul, "I can do all things through Christ who strengtheneth me." We do not conquer because we are strong, but because God is faithful to those who put their trust in Him. The fire of temptation cannot hurt us if we walk with God, for then we learn His way, and His will becomes ours. We must employ the weapons of defense which He has provided for us. A persistent and daily use of the Word of God, which is the "sword of the Spirit," cannot be ignored. That is a minimum essential for any one who bears the name of Christ. Quiet hours of meditation every day, when we have opportunity to disentangle ourselves from temporal pursuits, are needful, too. And then, let us not forget to begin and end the day with prayer and complete surrender to the loving care of a providential heavenly Father. A blessed day will be assured, and a needful night of rest, free from the turmoil of a troubled conscience, shall be ours.

A Tenacious Faith

Then Jesus went thence, and departed into the coasts of Tyre and Sidon. And, behold, a woman of Canaan came out of the same coasts, and cried unto him, saying, Have mercy on me, O Lord, thou son of David; my daughter is grievously vexed with a devil. But he answered her not a word. And his disciples came and besought him, saying, Send her away; for she crieth after us. But he answered and said, I am not sent but unto the lost sheep of the house of Israel. Then came she and worshipped him, saying, Lord, help me. But he answered and said, It is not meet to take the children's bread, and to cast it to dogs. And she said, Truth, Lord: yet the dogs eat of the crumbs which fall from their masters' table. Then Jesus answered and said unto her, O woman, great is thy faith: be it unto thee even as thou wilt. And her daughter was made whole from that very hour. Matthew 15:21-28

THE Savior has abundantly established His mastery over Satan. Jesus met him in the wilderness and Satan was forced to recede. He meets him again today and the evil one reluctantly yields his prey. A Syro-Phœnician woman whose "daughter is grievously vexed by a devil" received His benefaction. The woman without a name pleaded for His help, and by her victorious faith she has been immortalized. What does a name matter as long as the soul is cared for?

Jesus had come into the extreme northwestern corner of Canaan, on the coast of Tyre and Sidon, in search of rest and retirement. His days were long, and the willing spirit exhausted Him. There was so much to be done—so many needed Him. Never did He turn anyone away who sincerely sought His help. Handicapped by a mortal frame He became wearied and tired, and was often forced to seek seclusion and rest. The malignant unbelief of the Jews added further burdens which made a little rest and repose needful. His weariness on this occasion must have approached utter exhaustion, because, according to one of the Evangelists, He had requested not to be disturbed.

This momentary withdrawal may be viewed as a forecast of what would eventually happen when the kingdom should be taken from the Jews and established among the Gentiles. The incident is a precursor of what ultimately transpires when the historic records of the chosen people are embittered by the most God-forsaken loneliness. These records are still being written by the race without a country. You cannot crucify your Savior and escape the inevitable. The loneliness and the weeping will abide until the prostrate people shall call upon the Name of Jesus for deliverance.

The rest Jesus needed never seemed to be forthcoming. Others' need for help was always greater than His need for rest. Even in that land of the Gentiles, news about Jesus had filtered through. The glory of His achievements had preceded Him.

Among those who had heard of His coming was a wretched mother whose daughter was tortured by an evil spirit. We are not told the nature or the form that the affliction assumed, but evidently her faculties were invaded by the demon who made out of her a willing servant. Environment had done much to produce her. Commerce and pleasure, purple and soft clothing occupied the attention of her race. Idolatry and adultery were the ravaging sins of her time. The evils of ancient commerce and trading centered at Tyre and Sidon. The daughter was a victim of the atmosphere in which she lived. Doubtless, she was tainted by the sin of her time. She was lost beyond control, and finally, exhausted and diseased by her sin, she became an easy prey to the devil. Fortunate, indeed, was her mother, that a ray from the Sun of Righteousness had reached the darkened home. Happy day when the news of the Messiah and His works penetrated the Canaanitish darkness.

It is the story of a mother who like Jacob of old wrestles with the Lord until the blessing she seeks is forthcoming. It is the story of a mother who innocently bears the sufferings of a wayward child. It is the story of a mother who persists in her appeals until the fragmentary faith wrenches from Jesus the help she sought for her daughter.

One of the world's greatest tragedies is the fact that so much suffering is borne vicariously. Here is the wayward son; but could any pain equal the agonies that wrench the hearts of the father and the mother? A boy is imprisoned, but the parents pay the penalty. The boys upon the battlefield are called upon to face death, but the unsung heroes remain at home. The parents give the best they possess to be slaughtered upon the battlefield. That is the price we have to pay for war. As long as we choose war we will have to pay and pay. Here are the parents stooping over a child that is seriously ill. Who can measure the beat of their hearts and understand the pain? Only those who themselves have endured the equivalent. But strangely enough such vicarious suffering may often bring us into closer touch with God. The woman from Canaan was driven by her need to seek the aid of Jesus. Nor was she disappointed. A new life began for her that day. I am sure that her daughter, too, became different. Maybe the whole community was changed.

However, the mother was called upon to face many discouragements before the help she pleaded for was forthcoming.

In the first place, Jesus did not wish to be disturbed, for Mark says, "Jesus entered into an house and would have no man know it." Can you imagine that she was able to see Jesus without facing the disciples and prevailing upon them to make that interview possible? You recall how the disciples complained about the mothers who brought their children to Jesus that He should touch them. Before Jesus could be reached in His seclusion she must have been compelled to consult the disciples. And maybe the weather-beaten fishermen of Galilee looked like a hard lot.

Then, too, I am sure she did not forget that she belonged to a different race. Could she, who was a Gentile, hope to get a hearing from one who was a Jew? She must scale that high national barrier. She ventured forth heroically. Maybe she reasoned within herself, "The worst that can happen to me is that the disciples of this strange Jesus may be asked to take me away." But again that dogged faith persisted. *She found Jesus.*

That is when her troubles really began. The cold, adamant attitude of Jesus was strange behavior for "One who came to seek and to save the lost." He didn't even answer her when she spoke to Him. Even the disciples observed the silence, and they grew impatient with Him—perhaps more than the wretched mother. Naturally they were annoyed by her presence, and they asked Jesus to send her away. Her entreaties were attracting too much attention. The whole group might become a public spectacle if she should continue. The woman might have felt then that she had made a mistake in coming. She might have reasoned that the help she sought could not be obtained here. But again that dogged faith does not yield.

Finally He speaks to her, but only to say, "I am not sent but to the lost sheep of the house of Israel." How high the wall of separation becomes. He had no responsibility for her. She did not matter much in His economy, so it seemed. The apparent coldness must have been a part of His mercy plan. Something within probably told her to go home and do the best she could for the child. But instead she came and worshipped Him, prostrating herself before Him and saying, "Lord help me." What great things a mother will do to help her child—what pain she will endure, what humiliation she will bear, what burdens she will carry! All for a demon-possessed daughter.

But her worst trial is still to come. Jesus turned to her and said, "It isn't meet to give the children's bread to the dogs." To most people, that would have sealed up all hope. She might have retorted angrily, but she didn't. There is no trace of bitterness or even of despair. She drew a new impulse from this added humiliation. If she were a dog she would eat the crumbs underneath the children's table. Luther says, "She conquered the Master on His own ground." Then came from the Master the sweetest words she had ever heard, "O woman, great is thy faith, be it unto thee even as thou wilt." And her daughter became well.

From the beginning this mother had sensed that only Jesus could be of any help. She had heard that He had power over the demons and that they were subject unto Him. She had suffered so at the hand of this demon, she had been so subject to his malice, that her heart was overwhelmed and broken. Something must be done. If she could interest Jesus in the case, the tyranny would be broken, and in this confidence lay the foundation of her success. She did not know much about Jesus, but she knew enough. A little knowledge with confidence is worth more than all the theological knowledge in the world without faith. The Syro-Phœnician woman was impelled and controlled by a mighty conviction. Never before, never afterward, did Jesus sojourn there, and she utilized the one and only opportunity she had of consulting Him. And she did well.

There are times when the Savior is near. Then great decisions have to be made. You see, opportunities that come, also go. There are times when great spiritual things are in the making, and a man by the grace of God can settle his destiny forever. That is a visitation from heaven. If anyone desires divine help, then he must accept it when the Savior is near.

There may be much to hinder our approaches to God. We have no claims upon Him, but there is always help and consolation when we do reach Him. He speaks a word and the storm is stilled, grievous vexations cease and burdened hearts rejoice. There is no home but He can bear its burdens, and no wounded heart that He cannot touch and heal.

Thoughts and
Attitudes Revealed

And he was casting out a devil, and it was dumb. And it came to pass, when the devil was gone out, the dumb spake; and the people wondered. But some of them said, He casteth out devils through Beelzebub the chief of the devils. And others, tempting him, sought of him a sign from heaven. But he, knowing their thoughts, said unto them, Every kingdom divided against itself is brought to desolation; and a house divided against a house falleth. If Satan also be divided against himself, how shall his kingdom stand? because ye say that I cast out devils through Beelzebub. And if I by Beelzebub cast out devils, by whom do your sons cast them out? therefore shall they be your judges. But if I with the finger of God cast out devils, no doubt the kingdom of God is come upon you. When a strong man armed keepeth his palace, his goods are in peace: but when a stronger than he shall come upon him, and overcome him, he taketh from him all his armour wherein he trusted, and divideth his spoils. He that is not with me is against me: and he that gathereth not with me scattereth. When the unclean spirit is gone out of a man, he walketh through dry places, seeking rest; and finding none, he saith, I will return unto my house whence I came out. And when he cometh, he findeth it swept and garnished. Then goeth he, and taketh to him seven other spirits more wicked than himself; and they enter in, and dwell there: and the last state of that man is worse than the first.

And it came to pass, as he spake these things, a certain woman of the company lifted up her voice, and said unto him, Blessed is the womb that bare thee, and the paps which thou hast sucked. But he said, Yea rather, blessed are they that hear the word of God, and keep it.

Luke 11:14-28

L ENT introduces us to many subjects that are not pleasant; but a calm, prayerful consideration of all the incidents related to the passion of our Lord will be profitable. A dissertation on sin and its ultimate conclusion might strike a discordant note, but how will you be able to appreciate the symphonic melodies poured out from the cross if you have not first heard the utter disharmony created by sin in its ceaseless refrain? The better we understand the prevailing ills, the more we shall praise the One who came to set us free.

Then, as now, Jesus went out and leveled every barrier and defeated Satan and his henchmen at every turn. This conflict He waged in our behalf. "He was wounded for our transgressions, bruised for our iniquities. The chastisement of our peace was upon him, and with his stripes we are healed."

It was hard for Him to stand virtually friendless, to be humiliated and thorn-crowned as the raucous rabble hailed Him king. But Jesus saw humanity in bondage, harassed by a slavery as abject as only Satan could impose. He did it all for us.

The particular case of suffering referred to in our text is one in which the demons of darkness took possession of a wretched soul and made out of it "a habitation of dragons"—made it an instrument of evil and a victim of malicious obsession. A human being had been invaded by a spirit of the underworld which robbed him of his hearing and speech. The picture is tragic and pathetic.

Now every unregenerate man is under the dominion of evil. And the kingdom of evil is universal; it constitutes an empire as vast as the earth. Sin invariably blinds the eyes, seals the ears and ties the tongue to everything that is spiritual, good, and noble. "The god of this world hath blinded the eyes of them that believe not." And they are as deaf as they are blind. The carnival of turmoil within their hearts has hushed the voice of God. Dumb and speechless, deaf and blind they are.

It is the office and plan of Christ to destroy this horrible dominion exercised by the evil one, and to give liberty, hearing, speech, and sight to those who have been enslaved. "For this purpose the Son of God was manifested, that he might destroy the works of the devil."

Here is the program of the Christian church: man shall see God, man shall hear God, and man shall praise God. "Christianity is a divine plan for the expulsion of Satan" and all his enslaving influence.

Christ's work demonstrates His fitness to fulfill this program. The potencies of the underworld were forced to yield to His sublime authority. We would naturally conclude, and rightly so, that His ministry would be acceptable. The reactions, however, were as widely different as day and night.

Christ faced many varying attitudes that day, and attitude is one of the most important factors in determining man's relationship to Christ. What we are is determined by our attitude. We are not measured by what we have done but by what we are. The pupil in the class room is graded more on his attitude than even the teacher knows. The man in the community may make many mistakes, but if he has the right attitude he is respected. The home, the community, the state, the church, all are watching our attitude. In short, the disposition in the heart of a man makes a world of difference. What is our attitude to Christ and the kingdom? Are we for Him or are we against Him? Do we gather or do we scatter?

Now the ministry of Jesus caused men to reveal certain dispositions. "He is set for a stone of stumbling that the thoughts of many hearts may be revealed." His presence always caused divisions.

Thus, it is related in the words of our text, "It came to pass when the devil was gone out, the dumb spake, and the people wondered." There are people who never get beyond the curiosity stage—they only marvel and then forget. These people were filled with amazement. They had seen a lot in their day but never such a thing as this. They were common people with common sense. It was from people such as these that Jesus chose His disciples. They were schooled in the ordinary works of life. According to Matthew these people began to wonder and ask, "Is not this the Son of David?" Conviction was taking root—they were for Him. What a following Jesus might have had among these people if the bitter, bigoted Pharisees had only left them alone! Their attitude was friendly, and what a difference that made.

But there were others, too, who witnessed the miracle. These were neither friendly nor reasonable. Rather than admit that Jesus was the Christ, they would insist upon an absurdity. The miracle they could not deny, and for all the world they could not discredit it or rule the incident out. So they said He had the help of the devil. "He casteth out devils by Beelzebub the chief of the devils." To what extremity those who are inimical will go! Their conclusion was ridiculous and illogical. But they did not deny the miracle. Many skeptics to-day deny all miracles. Theorizing about the impossibility of miracles is far out-weighed by the testimony of eye-witnesses. Yet the difficulty of performing miracles is set up as a sort of bogey man by those who do not believe. If we believe that there is a God we can also believe in the supernatural. He can stop the sun in its perennial course if He chooses to do so; He can turn night into day if He likes; He can crash the universe if He so desires. Let us not measure God's power by our limitations.

Jesus proceeds to expose the fallacy employed by these men in their reasoning. "If Satan cast out Satan, he is divided against himself, and how shall his kingdom stand? . . . Every kingdom divided against itself is brought to desolation, and a house divided against a house falleth." His accusers were silent; there wasn't much they could say. Their lack of common sense and coherent thought had already made trouble for them. Their attitude was bad.

But that day there was still another group that observed the miracle. These people were ready to believe *if* a sign from heaven would help to substantiate the validity of all His claims. So they asked for a sign from heaven. It seems they already had seen a sign, but that didn't help them. They would haunt the Son of God and pursue Him from

one corner of Canaan to the other, asking and de-
manding signs, and yet His whole ministry was a
sign. Set a new sun in the sky, create a new constellation, or produce some heavenly display "so that
a man though a fool might read as he runs."
Would that have satisfied them? No! They had the
Scriptures, and they wouldn't believe them. Since
they wouldn't believe "Moses and the prophets"
(so Jesus said in His parable of the rich man and
Lazarus), they wouldn't believe if a man returned
from the dead to say it was true. From hemisphere to hemisphere, from pole to pole, they
would have driven the Lord to satisfy their in-
quisitorial curiosity. If a man will not believe, you
cannot compel him to believe. He might yield for
the sake of expediency, "but a man convinced
against his will is of the same opinion still." Christ
saw the enmity within. These men were not for
Him. Hesitation in their case meant opposition,
and their lack of judgment was positive guilt.
"He that is not with me is against me."

On this occasion only one voice was clearly
lifted on behalf of Jesus. "As he spake these things
a certain woman of the company lifted up her
voice and said, Blessed is the womb that bare thee."
Just one acclaiming voice out of that milling,
mottled throng. In a bitter and hateful atmosphere, that one voice must have meant much to
Jesus. She spoke as a mother, and she spoke well.

She thought, How happy must a mother be who has such a son—one honored by men who are truly good, one to whom many are indebted, one on whom many eyes are turned and from whom much is expected. She knew how a mother's happiness is bound up with the children she has carried and nursed and reared. Maybe her own children had not fared so well. There are so many ways that wind and wind, so many things that can happen to the children we love and for whom we covet so much. Some disappointments every mother must bear, but some seem to have nothing but sorrows. Many a Hebrew mother had perhaps secretly coveted the place of Mary, the mother of Jesus. This woman gave utterance, truly, to the desire of every mother.

But there is even a higher blessedness, a still more surpassing gladness that might be shared alike by Hebrew and Gentile mothers. Jesus answered, "Blessed are they that hear the Word of God and keep it." There is the royal road to victorious joy—the way to blessedness. True happiness lies so near at hand. Have you found it?

O may these heavenly pages be
My ever dear delight;
And still new beauties may I see,
And still increasing light.

Divine Instructor, gracious Lord!
Be Thou forever near:
Teach me to love Thy sacred Word,
And view my Savior there.

The Christian religion is built upon something
more substantial than mere sentiment; though it
is beyond me, how any one could really be gripped
by the Word of God and yet remain without any
semblance of sentiment. There must certainly be
a certain amount of feeling in the heart of a man
who will, if need be, forsake all things and follow
Jesus. The Gospel accepted and lived is a true expression of Christianity. It is not enough just to
belong to Bethlehem or any other congregation. It
is not enough just to admire Gothic structure
which mellows so richly with the passing years.
That may be praiseworthy, but Christianity requires more than admiration. It requires adher-
ence and obedience to the Word of God. If we are
lacking in those qualities, vaulted ceilings and
Gothic arches will do little for us. It is not enough
to say that we have a ritual handed down to us by
our fathers, though it be a beautiful ritual, embel-
lished with tradition and ancient love. Personal
faith and devotion to the divine Will is the essential quality, and we may have that without any
ritual. Christianity cannot be ascribed to tangible
forms. These may help us by providing a common

vehicle for congregational expression. Those alone are truly blessed who are diligent in hearing God's Word, who treasure it in their hearts, and who place all their hope in it.

Abundant Provisions

After these things Jesus went over the sea of Galilee, which is the sea of Tiberias. And a great multitude followed him, because they saw his miracles which he did on them that were diseased. And Jesus went up into a mountain, and there he sat with his disciples. And the passover, a feast of the Jews, was nigh.

When Jesus then lifted up his eyes, and saw a great company come unto him, he saith unto Philip, Whence shall we buy bread, that these may eat? And this he said to prove him: for he himself knew what he would do. Philip answered him, Two hundred pennyworth of bread is not sufficient for them, that every one of them may take a little. One of his disciples, Andrew, Simon Peter's brother, saith unto him. There is a lad here, which hath five barley loaves, and two small fishes: but what are they among so many? And Jesus said, Make the men sit down. Now there was much grass in the place. So the men sat down, in number about five thousand. And Jesus took the loaves; and when he had given thanks, he distributed to the disciples, and the disciples to them that were set down; and likewise of the fishes as much as they would. When they were filled, he said unto his disciples, Gather up the fragments that remain, that nothing be lost.

Therefore they gathered them together, and filled twelve baskets with the fragments of the five barley loaves, which remained over and above unto them that had eaten. Then those men, when they had seen the miracle that Jesus did, said, This is of a truth that prophet that should come into the world. John 6:1-15

THE incident in our text is a factual demonstration of what Jesus taught in the Sermon on the Mount when He said, "Seek ye first the kingdom of God and all these things shall be added unto you." All good things come unto those who seek God first.

There were many who were drawn to Jesus. He was recognized as a great personality. The miraculous power which He exhibited so frequently touched them with a strange and persuasive force. They had listened intently to His truthful and searching sermons. There was something so strangely divine about His manner of preaching and His finality in the art of interpreting the Scriptures. The Messianic hope crystallized and became real to them when they listened to Jesus. They would go long distances to hear Him. He would appear in the cities, villages and towns, in the countryside or even in the wilderness, and large numbers of anxious, seeking souls always gathered around Him. Maybe their Messianic notions were confused and chaotic. After years of misinterpretation by their so-called leaders and teachers it would have been strange indeed if their understanding of the Messiah and His mission had been clearly defined. The prevailing enthusiasm for Jesus and His ministry thrills us more than we can say. How much they really needed Him perhaps they never understood. Only a few continued to absorb His benevolent counsel.

All alike needed Him. Men and women and children followed Him, forgetting their own comfort and convenience to be near Him. They were seeking the kingdom of which He spoke and of which they knew so little. On this particular occasion Jesus had gone into the wilderness to get a much needed rest, but the multitudes learned of His retreat and followed Him. The persistence of their search must have pleased Christ. In any event He honored their persistence as He so often did by supplying all their needs. Their earnest desire kindled His great compassion and the glory of God was again manifested. Christ's wonder-working grace was set in motion.

Jesus was often frustrated in His work by wickedness and evil, but these faithful followers were not against Him. Every sacrifice made to follow Him seriously and sincerely was, and always will be, compensated a thousand times. The way is sometimes hard, abrupt, and circuitous. There will be seas to circumvent, deserts to face, and labors to be wrought. But the end will be good.

The multitudes today, as in the time of Jesus, may be sinful. Each one knows best his own need. I am thankful for the throngs that worship in our churches, for the thousands that fill our sanctuaries to overflowing. This happens Sunday after Sunday until it has become perennial. Man's crying need finds expression here as nowhere else. Something has gone wrong, and consciously or unconsciously, the nation, the commonwealth, the community, and the individual seek their refuge there. God bless them for seeking the remedy there. Where else could it be found? They may not know much, but they do know that the church can help them and shelter those who are in need. They come to listen for the footfalls of the Master and to hear the voice of God. They may represent a chaotic crowd seeking the Lord as did the multitudes in the wilderness. Their thinking may be confused. They may not fully understand the seriousness of their own condition, and perhaps they understand even less about the Lord and His mission. But they are there, and woe unto the man who feeds them stones when they cry for bread. God be merciful to the man who sends the surging multitudes away unsatisfied. To proclaim anything but Christ to them is only to laugh at their impotence, and hatred instead of love is engendered in their hearts. The great masses that assemble for worship are still saying, "We would see Jesus."

Jesus Himself dealt kindly with those who came seeking Him. Should we do less?

Just as everything is not right with the multitude, so we discover that not all is right, even with the disciples. How frail and faulty faith may sometimes be. What havoc the need for human necessities has wrought upon some hearts. What shall we eat, wherewithal shall we be clothed, where shall we find shelter? Have the disciples forgotten that our kind, providential heavenly Father will supply their needs? Philip wondered how the masses could be fed in the wilderness. You and I would likely have been troubled, too. Reason had no answer. Two hundred pennyworth of bread—five barley loaves and two small fishes. The supply was not adequate; it could not be done. So the disciples of Jesus suggested that He send the people home. At least that solution was possible, and it was reasonable. Philip and Andrew spoke for us. Doesn't it seem to you that they were right? Wouldn't you have acted the same way under those circumstances? How little the disciples knew about Jesus. Had they known more, faith would have triumphed over every misgiving they might have had. They really never had experienced His power and goodness. Yes, they believed, but they looked at their own helplessness when they should have observed the unlimited resources from which Jesus could draw.

We make the same mistake when we are overwhelmed by the enormity of our sins. It is hard for us to imagine that "where sin is abundant, grace is yet more abundant." Would God cast us aside because we cannot understand? Jesus did not turn men away because they were overwhelmed. He was always patient with those who were slow of heart to believe. He continued to bless them with His presence until they finally understood.

Our faith is often tested when we stand face to face with social or economic problems. What can we do to avert disaster when the supplies are low and privation lurks around the corner? Poverty brings back many bitter memories of misgivings and apprehension. Surely He who fed the multitudes in the desert wilderness can care for you and those you love. Let us not yield to perplexity and despair. Whatever the emergency may be, He has abundant supplies to meet our needs, whether they are material or spiritual. "Behold the fowls of the air, for they sow not, neither do they reap or gather into barns, yet your heavenly Father feedeth them. Are ye not much better than they? Behold the lilies of the field, they toil not, neither do they spin. Yet Solomon in all his glory was not arrayed like one of these."

The church is called upon to face much the same problem. The sea of wickedness stretches

from one end of the world to the other. We find
it everywhere, and everywhere sin seems to be in
the ascendency. Paganism has improved while
Christianity often gives a poor account of its faith.
What impact can the church make against such a
mass of iniquity? What is the use of expending our
energies in a cause that seems to be losing? According to human calculations, there is not much
that can be done. But the church, the repository
of God's economy, however frail and faulty it may
be, has penetrating powers which permeate, re-
store, and regenerate. Reason again says, "Your
ministrations cannot reach very far." To us that
may seem to be true. But it is equally true that we
can reach some. Why send out a few missionaries
when the fields are so vast and the harvest is white?
Because we can reach some and share with them
the good provided by the church. Filth and squal-
or, disease and despair they know too well. Would
you help them if you could? If you knew that only
one family could be reached wouldn't you still be
willing to help? Enslaved under the fear of a
mysterious god, crushed under a system of super-
stition which requires sacrifices that break and
impoverish, these people who live in darkness are
eternally unhappy. Can we help them? Yes, by
telling them the truth. And as our interest and
sympathy grow, our support will increase, and the
missionaries will multiply and the fruits shall be

abundant. Practically all of the civilized world today is a product of that spirit.

Jesus says, "The poor ye have always with you." There are many who need food and clothing and shelter. These multitudes frighten us. What can we do to help so many in need? The answer is: much, if our hearts are right. We must bring them close to us to really understand their need. You have plenty at your house. The children have never cried for bread or begged for shelter. Nearly always you have been able to supply more than the mere essentials. We should be thankful that our children are well fed, well clothed and well housed. But there will always be some concern for those not so fortunate. In the next house may be a family in poor circumstances. The reasons for their poverty may be many and varied, but children are children still, and to see them crying for crusts is heartrending. Those children hounded by poverty are just as precious as yours. They like good things to eat and nice things to wear, just as much as your children do. Their father has struggled with unemployment at times, or with sickness that incapacitated him so that the income was cut short; the savings were soon expended in doctor and hospital bills and stark poverty began to stalk where plenty had always prevailed. You would help if you could, wouldn't you? And by the grace of God it will actually seem that what you have left will take you farther and bring you more joy because you were kind to someone. You could not help all who needed you, perhaps, but if others did what you were doing, all would be provided for. What you have always multiplies when it is used in God's Name.

What about the unworthy poor? I suppose there are some; unworthy poor stand out like monstrosities. Have you ever seen a child that was unworthy? Have you ever seen a mother struggling to keep her little brood alive who was unworthy? Have you ever seen a sick one who was unworthy? Jesus must have loved the unworthy ones because He always helped them. I remember, too, that before God I was not worthy, yet God graciously took care of me. There was nothing to commend me, but the mercy of God reaches far.

It is really remarkable how much can be accomplished when all hearts work together for the good of the kingdom. The areas to be reached may be vast and widespread, the hindrances may seem impassable, the means inadequate; yet the impact of one act of kindness may eventually be felt to the ends of the earth.

The Ages Are Telling

And in the sixth month the angel Gabriel was sent from God unto a city of Galilee, named Nazareth, to a virgin espoused to a man whose name was Joseph, of the house of David; and the virgin's name was Mary. And the angel came in unto her, and said, Hail thou that art highly favoured, the Lord is with thee: blessed art thou among women. And when she saw him, she was troubled at his saying, and cast in her mind what manner of salutation this should be. And the angel said unto her, Fear not, Mary: for thou hast found favour with God. And, behold, thou shalt conceive in thy womb, and bring forth a son, and shalt call his name JESUS. He shall be great, and shall be called the Son of the Highest: and the Lord God shall give unto him the throne of his father David: And he shall reign over the house of Jacob for ever; and of his kingdom there shall be no end. Then said Mary unto the angel, How shall this be, seeing I know not a man? And the angel answered and said unto her, The Holy Ghost shall come upon thee, and the power of the Highest shall overshadow thee: therefore also that holy thing which shall be born of thee shall be called the Son of God. And, behold, thy cousin Elisabeth, she hath also

*conceived a son in her old age: and this is the sixth
month with her, who was called barren. For with God
nothing shall be impossible. And Mary said, Behold the
handmaid of the Lord; be it unto me according to thy
word. And the angel departed from her.*   Luke 1:26-38

THE children of God waited a long time before
the words of Jehovah God, uttered in Paradise, were fulfilled. "The seed of the woman shall
bruise the serpent's head." The day of fulfillment
would be a terrible one. Then the Savior would be
wounded, and Satan's power would be destroyed.
Generations waited and went the way of the world.
The scrolls that held the mysterious promise became grey with age. Dynasties changed and for-
eign powers levied their toll. Egypt, Assyria, Per-
sia, Babylon, and Rome all had a part in the preparation for the coming of God's Servant. But now
the ages are filled, pregnant with celestial excitement. The Liberator, the Destroyer of evil, the
Savior of mankind, who had been promised so early and who was the burden of so many subsequent
prophecies, is about to appear.

His approach is not marked by any particular
glory. Many other occasions had been more auspi-
cious and the circumstances far more favorable.
There had been times when the Hebrew people
were independent and prosperous, when the house
of David flourished and the promises of God and

their fulfillment seemed so imminent. But clearly, man's helplessness is God's opportunity. After four thousand years of preparatory work among the Gentiles and the Jews, the world is ready for the most supreme historic incident, not only of that century but of all centuries. The significance of the Messiah's coming would revolutionize all relationships, and the birth of the King of kings would, in the words of Carlyle, "lift the gates of empires off their hinges, and turn the stream of centuries into new channels." Hereafter all things would be dated B.C and A.D.

God did not need to hurry His plan, for with Him "a thousand years is as one day." His plans will never fail, and with Him there is no miscarriage of justice. Time and again it seemed that the people of God would be obliterated. Wars, slaveries, and captivities overwhelmed them, but God always preserved a remnant in which, and through which, His promise might be fulfilled. He moves mysteriously to bring His plans to fruition, through prosperity and through adversity. He cultivates the good and noble—and destroys the ignoble. He saves the wheat and scatters the chaff.

The remnants that returned from the Babylonian captivity under Nehemiah were a purged people, but in numbers the real Hebrews were not many. God was able to preserve the antecedents of the Christ, and the Messiah who came was clearly consonant with the ancient patriarchal-prophetic promise.

The early promise of a Messiah first uttered in Paradise was vague and general. From whence He should stem, save that He was to be born of a woman, was not revealed. Eve anticipated that the promised Savior of mankind might be born to her. But years passed and the race was dispersed and nations were formed, and out of these God selected one people to be His chosen care. He selected Abraham, the Son of Terah in Ur, to become the father of the faithful ones. But the promise was still general when it was reiterated to Isaac and to Jacob.

The process of sifting and narrowing down would be a long one. To Israel the promise was uttered and out of Israel to Judea. The city of Bethlehem was designated as the birthplace of the Christ. The circle became smaller and smaller as the years passed, and then like a flash from a clear sky the angel of God appeared before Mary in Nazareth and the divine favor of becoming the mother of Jesus devolved upon her. No prophetic voice had been heard for four hundred years, and the scribes diligently studied the promises of the past in hope of discerning the time and place and the manner of His coming. He came when He was not expected. They were looking for another.

From Nazareth He came, a little town, out of

the way, despised, disreputable, called the Galilee of the Gentiles. As Abraham and David rejoiced to be assured that the Messiah would be a direct descendant, so much more illustrious is the privilege of becoming the mother of Jesus. We do not worship her, because "Thou shalt worship the Lord God alone." Nor do we pray to her or in her name, but we do honor her for the distinction which came to her—for her holiness and for her obedience to God.

Why could not some person of prominence have been selected? Why not someone near of kin to the Pharisees, the scribes or the high priest? At the time Jesus was born, all these classes represented corruption. Mary represented the pure and undefiled, the faithful adherents of the ancient promises. In the second place, God uses the poor and humble to shame the great in the eternal processes of His kingdom. Lastly, the mother of Jesus must be of the house of Jacob and of David's lineage.

Why should a virgin birth have been necessary for the Messiah? Frankly, I answer that we do not know. But we might also ask, Why not? Surely God's plans will not be brought into question because He chose a virgin for the distinguished office of being the mother of Jesus. We are not called upon to explain the mystery. It is only one of many mysteries, and to deny any of them would be to do violence to the Word of God. That cannot be modified or altered.

Seven hundred years before the birth of Christ Isaiah, the evangelical prophet, peering into the future, had foretold the event. Here are his words: "Behold a virgin shall conceive and bear a son, and shall call his name Immanuel." That the angel Gabriel should come to Nazareth in Galilee and proclaim to a virgin betrothed to Joseph that she should be the mother of Jesus, seems utterly unreasonable. But the supernatural cannot be rationalized. "Why the laws of nature were partially set aside in the birth of Isaac and John the Baptist, who both were born out of season we cannot explain, much less the divine act which set aside totally the laws of nature and by a creative act formed the Son of God in the bosom of a virgin." The mystery will be revealed in the church triumphant, and then we will understand the incarnation, the atonement, and the dual personality as well.

The virgin birth about which there has always been so much bitter controversy is the greatest miracle ever wrought. To those who believe, Mary will always stand a representative of the best, the purest, and the noblest in womanhood. She matured in the same environment as the other women of her time and was called upon to face the prevailing temptations, but she withstood them and remained pure and undefiled. The unbelief of her time is almost incomprehensible, rising at times in violent persecutions; but in spite of it all, in the face of ignorance and violence, she clung to the ancient promises and cherished the prophecies uttered to Israel. Utterly oblivious to the part she would have in the incarnation of God's Son, she was ready when the messenger of God announced to her the disposition of the divine counsel. "Behold the handmaid of the Lord, be it unto me according to thy word." She attained the crown of womanhood, the highest achievement of motherhood, when she found favor with God. They are truly great who remain faithful to their Lord and Master, whose personal interests remain subservient to the will of God. Whoever they are, wherever they may be, whatever may be their inclinations, it is always, "Lord, what wouldst Thou have me do."

Mary was troubled, but her troubles issued in joy. The stigmata of wagging tongues when they referred to her virgin birth, and the sword that pierced her soul when they hanged her Son upon a tree, were overshadowed by the resurrection joy. The women who came early to the grave were weeping as they gave way to the weight of sorrow, but their troubles became a great joy when the angel told them of the resurrection of Jesus. The shepherds keeping watch over their flocks by night were fearful and troubled when the heavens were opened and angel messengers filled the sky with songs, but when they went to Bethlehem to see the things that had come to pass and found the Christ-child there, they were glad, and the effervescent troubles issued in joy.

Thus the Lord of a million worlds became a native of the earth. He became one of us and assumed the joys and the sorrows common to man. His interest in a special way thereby centered in our corner of the universe. He laid aside momentarily the toils of a universal empire "that He might mediate and consummate our welfare." He took upon Himself our human nature that He might thus be enabled to impart to us His divine nature.

> Welcome to earth, Thou noble guest,
> Through whom the sinful world is blest!
> Thou com'st to share our misery,
> What can we render, Lord, to Thee!
>
> Were earth a thousand times as fair,
> Beset with gold and jewels rare,
> She yet were far too poor to be
> A narrow cradle, Lord, for Thee.

A Universal King

And when they drew nigh unto Jerusalem, and were come to Bethphage, unto the mount of Olives, then sent Jesus two disciples, saying unto them, Go into the village over against you, and straightway ye shall find an ass tied, and a colt with her: loose them, and bring them unto me. And if any man say ought unto you, ye shall say, The Lord hath need of them; and straightway he will send them. All this was done, that it might be fulfilled which was spoken by the prophet, saying, Tell ye the daughter of Sion, Behold, thy King cometh unto thee, meek, and sitting upon an ass, and a colt the foal of an ass. And the disciples went, and did as Jesus commanded them, and brought the ass, and the colt, and put on them their clothes, and they set him thereon. And a very great multitude spread their garments in the way; others cut down branches from the trees, and strawed them in the way. And the multitudes that went before, and that followed, cried, saying, Hosanna to the son of David: Blessed is he that cometh in the name of the Lord; Hosanna in the highest. Matthew 21:1-9

" JESUS of Nazareth, King of the Jews," Pilate wrote in the superscription upon the cross. The Jews resented it and asked Pilate to change the superscription. He aptly and abruptly answered, "What I have written, I have written." Jesus was even more a king than Pilate knew, for He was the Lord of lords and the King of kings. Jesus of Nazareth held a scepter that was universal. Powers unlimited were vested in Him, so that He reigned *ad infinitum*. Every planet in the vast created system, every star, every constellation, every galaxy of created things reaching out into the peripheral limits of eternity, was obedient to His beck and call. Never would they see another like Him until the end of time, when He will return in the clouds with great power and glory.

Jesus never claimed to be a statesman, though His inherent wisdom could have found solutions for the national and the international problems precipitated by the counsel of foolish men. He was not a militant general in shimmering official regalia, surrounded by a bodyguard of armed men and supported by an army of willing soldiers. How Peter secured the sword with which he cut off the ear of the servant of the high priest in the Garden of Gethsemane no one knows. There was another sword, too, but who owned it or where it came from we are not told. All we know is that Jesus said to Peter, "Put up again thy sword in his place, for all they that take the sword shall perish by the sword." That was all. We hear no more about it. Jesus was not known as a scholar, though sometimes people wondered that He who hadn't studied books knew so much. He was just a poor man with calloused hands that told of toil and honest labor, and "He had no form nor comeliness that they should desire him."

He knew that He was a king and moved with the dignity and the authority of a monarch, wherever the circumstances required His presence. From Nazareth to Calvary He was moved and inspired by the greatness and nobility of His kingship and heavenly parentage. God is my Father and I am His Son. "All things are given me of my Father, that all should honor the Son as they honor the Father." Listen to His prayer: "Father, glorify thou me with the glory I had with thee before the world was."

Even when Jesus stood before the august assemblage called the Sanhedrin He did not waver in the conception of His kingly office. Before Pontius Pilate, the Roman procurator, He admitted that He was a king and that He had come into the world to be a king, but He added: "My kingdom is not of this world." To the high priest who adjured Him in the name of the living God He answered, "Thou hast said that I am."

We are thankful that the voice of the people

has prevailed in our United States, so that we do not have to bow and scrape to kings with their royal retinue. Europe has paraded her kings in gold and silver and purple, accompanied by escorts of decorated men, but what a price her people have paid and are paying today, upon battlefields drenched in bloody gore.

On Palm Sunday there was no glory, no ceremony, no proud superiority when the King of kings made His triumphal entry into the Holy City. It was a homely and lowly incident. Jesus entered the portals of the ancient city riding upon an ass and the foal of an ass,—surrounded by Galilean fishermen, bearded and weatherbeaten, who had braved the waves of Tiberias often in peril of their lives. Around this little retinue were gathered multitudes of lowly peasants and their children, waving palm branches, the symbol of victory and conquest, and spreading their coarse homespun garments on the way. It is a beautiful picture in all its simple majesty, foreshadowing events yet to come. There was a song in the air that day. Jerusalem had never heard it before, except when their priests intoned the ancient promises. The mighty escort was singing as it wound its way into Jerusalem, "Hosanna to the Son of David; Blessed is he that cometh in the name of the Lord; Hosanna in the highest." Never before had Jerusalem been so moved. The foundation stones trembled under the weight of His divine glory. The people said, "Who is this?" And the multitudes answered, "This is Jesus the prophet of Nazareth in Galilee."

To Jesus the day was one of demonstration, when unseen powers were released and the people acclaimed Him King. To the disciples, as they recalled the three years of His official ministry which they had shared, it must have been an unforgetable, a red-letter day. It was an armistice—a momentary cessation of hostilities to provide a respite for the Master as He hurried to Calvary's pain and turmoil. The memories of such a day would help steel the disciples, too, for the ensuing conflict which would momentarily overwhelm them. From Palm Sunday to Easter would constitute a momentous week. It has no equivalent anywhere in the annals of men.

Jesus loved the history and the traditions of His own people. In part, at least, He was a product of these. But in His interpretation of the Scriptures He spoke with such assurance and finality that the people were amazed. He spoke as a divine King. "Ye have heard that it hath been said, An eye for an eye. . . . But I say unto you, That ye resist not evil. . . . Ye have heard that it hath been said, Thou shalt love thy neighbor, and hate thine enemy. . . . But I say unto you, Love your enemies." "Whosoever heareth these sayings of mine, and doeth them, I will liken him unto a wise man, who built his house upon a rock." Jesus stood before the lame man and said to him, "Be of good cheer, thy sins are forgiven thee." To the leper He said, "Be thou cleansed," and the ghostly whiteness became the ruddy flush of health. To the boisterous sea that foamed and swelled He said, "Peace be still." And even the elements obeyed Him, for the angry waves subsided. He stood in the presence of the dead and they arose; life returned to possess the empty frame. He spoke and His command was obeyed, just as when He uttered the divine fiat into the uncreated void and darkness fled and light flooded all things.

The people wondered. The wind and the waves yielded Him their obedience. He commanded the evil spirits and even they obeyed Him and yielded their prey. Surely, they thought, His coming is a visitation from God. Others took up stones to destroy Him, and the stones fell helplessly from their hands. The mob spirit flared and burned fiercely when the people from Nazareth took Him up into a mountain to thrust Him down. But the Evangelist says, "He walking through the midst of them went his way." They seemed helpless to do Him any harm.

There was much enthusiasm for Jesus on Palm Sunday. They wanted to take Him by force and make Him king. He could break the yoke of Rome and create for them a glorious nation. But when they looked for Him He was gone. The leaders of the people, however, were not enthusiastic. They hated Him fiercely. They began to make a case against Him. Charges were freely flung. "He eats with publicans and sinners; he is a glutton and a wine bibber; he drives out evil spirits by the help of Beelzebub." But all their charges availed nothing, so they resorted to violence. They plotted to arrest Him and get Him out of the way, but those sent to arrest Him returned empty-handed. "Arrest him? No man has ever spoken as he does." Finally, they agreed He should die—the high priest had so suggested. The Passover was being celebrated, and there were many people milling around. They could not find Him. They said He was afraid, and they gave orders that anyone who saw Him should report it and He would forthwith be arrested.

It was at this moment that a strange company, followed by the singing hosts, was winding its way down the slopes of Olivet. Bitterness burned at white heat in the hearts of His enemies, but He rode peacefully and majestically into the city. "Dogs will bark at the moon," and Satan's friends will curse the King of kings. As yet, the Christ is unmoved and unmolested. He led the way for this mottled Palm Sunday crowd as they moved toward the temple, and there He stopped long enough to cast out the money changers who had made it a

den of thieves. Then He spoke to the scribes and
the Pharisees. To these it became a memorable
Sunday. "Woe unto you scribes and Pharisees. You
are thieves, you have devoured defenceless widows'
houses. You are whited sepulchres, full of vileness.
You are vipers and you are bent for hell." No one
had dared to speak thus before, and the enemies
stormed and fumed and plotted anew His destruction. Finally, they thought they had succeeded.
They nailed Him to a tree.

The cross upon which He hung has become
a beneficent emblem and has stretched forth its
perennial welcome to sin-burdened souls the world
over. He suffered there for the sins of the world,
He broke the power of death and rendered Satan
powerless as He established and secured the kingdom of God. Jehovah's decree was satisfied, and
the shadows of the past had become reality. "Thou
art my Son, this day have I begotten thee. Ask of
me, and I will give thee the nations for thine in-
heritance, and the uttermost part of the earth for
thy possession."

He shall be a king forevermore. Follow your
King through the portals of Jerusalem, sit with
Him at the communion table on Maundy Thurs-
day, follow to Calvary on Good Friday and see
Him die there. Watch Nicodemus and Joseph of
Arimathea tenderly lay His body in Joseph's grave,
worshipping quietly on the Sabbath day. And re-

turn to the sepulchre on Easter Day, when the
angels shall proclaim the resurrection of the King.

> All hail the power of Jesus' name,
> Let angels prostrate fall.
> Bring forth the royal diadem
> And crown Him Lord of all.

The angels praise Him with cherubic and se-
raphic songs, and this refrain is ringing to heaven's
end. "Holy, holy, holy is the Lord, the earth is
full of His glory." The ransomed hosts shall praise
Him with celestial songs until the corridors of
their heavenly home echo with resounding praise.
Dying sinners who have stumbled to the cross as
their last refuge yearn withal that they might have
a thousand tongues with which to sing their Redeemer's praise.

Shall we stand silently by, while the heavens resound, little clods of earth that we are—trifling
fragments of God's magnificent universe? Open
wide the doors of your heart, and the King of
glory shall come in!

The church needs a living membership, people
who will not yield the citadel of the heart because
Christ the King is regnant there—men and women
who will fight to keep their royal heritage un-
touched by hands that are defiled. The church
needs members who will say, "Take all that I have,

my property, my friends, my position and all that I possess—strip me of all that men hold dear, and I shall still be singing, 'Praise God from whom all blessings flow.' Drive me to despair and send me to tortures if you can, but I shall raise my hand and salute the Christ my King."

When I survey the wondrous cross
On which the King of glory died,
My richest gain I count but loss,
And pour contempt on all my pride.

Were the whole realm of nature mine,
That were a tribute far too small;
Love so amazing, so divine,
Demands my soul, my life, my all.

The Cross My Glory

But God forbid that I should glory, save in the cross of our Lord Jesus Christ, by whom the world is crucified unto me, and I unto the world. Galatians 6:14

PAUL had established many churches. He was a man with a far flung ministry, who planted the cross in all the cultured centers touching the great sea. He flung the crucifix on the banquet table of the gods and challenged the philosophies of Greece and Rome. Some thought he was mad, others thought he was moved by a fanatical zeal, but some there were—wherever he preached—who accepted his message about a crucified Savior, and a congregation always remained as a witness to the praise and glory of the Name he proclaimed. From Corinth to Galatia to Ephesus to Philippi to Colosse, to Thessalonica and Rome—there you have the itinerary of Saul of Tarsus who became Paul the Apostle to the Gentiles. Blessed with a faith that was exuberant and strong, he feared nothing. No power on earth or under the earth could dissuade him once he had heard the call to service. "I can do all things through Christ who strengtheneth me." That was his conviction. And a man who has that much faith is hard to stop.

The forces of evil sundered by hatreds and selfish desires were united in their efforts to destroy him and the strange gospel that he ventured to preach. The enemies made common cause in the elimination of Paul's influence which threatened to destroy their position and standing. He was bound and scourged and imprisoned, but the indomitable spirit of Paul could not be fettered. Whether in prison or out of it he was still Paul.

The Judaisers were sure to follow his trail, and wherever they went they brought discord and division to the Christians. They beguiled the disciples of Paul by principles subversive to the Gospel. They robbed the Savior of the glory ascribed to Him by Paul. They sought to supplement the work that Christ had wrought upon the cross. In other words, what the Savior had done was not enough. "Except ye be circumcised after the manner of Moses ye cannot be saved." Salvation, according to their logic, could not be provided alone by the cross. The cross, plus something else which they could provide, would supply their needed salvation. They were afraid to ascribe too much power to the cross lest they might offend the Christians of Jewish origin. They would seek to hide the cross. But for Paul the cross was everything—nothing must be permitted to overshadow it or to replace it. "God forbid that I should glory save in the cross of our Lord Jesus Christ."

The cross as a divine fact has been and still is the distinguishing characteristic of the Christian religion. If you leave out the cross, or permit it to be overshadowed, then Christianity is obliterated, too. The cross is the gospel. All the prophecies, all the commandments, all the promises, and all the joys of the Christian faith are cross-centered. It is out from the cross that the power of Christ radiates. To sinful men it will always remain a mystery. Human thought and language cannot compass it. We cannot know the cross as God knows it, but we can know what He has told us about it.

It is a far cry from the cross of Calvary, a symbol of shame and dishonor, to the cross employed today as an ornament or decoration to symbolize victory. We thank God for every cross that appears, in or on our churches today, because it proclaims a perennial message of a crucified and risen Savior.

How carefully the story of the crucifixion has been related by the holy writers! The time element is given due consideration, for Christ died upon the cross when Tiberius was emperor of Rome and Pontius Pilate was procurator in Judea. The cross is an established fact, a reality. Realities always deserve a fair hearing. But it is a fact which belongs to eternity as well, stretching from eternity to eternity. God had planned the cross "before the foundations of the world were laid."

When the plan begins to unfold itself within the Old Testament we can see how all things look forward to Calvary. All the roads found in the old dispensation converge upon the cross. All the prophets and patriarchs bore witness of the coming Christ. He is the center and the core of God's plan according to the revealed Word, and the very essence of the work which He wrought is to be found in the cross which stood like a silent sentinel on the barest and highest hill in all the world.

Let us study our Old Testament a little more diligently and it will lead us to Calvary. Let us not forget that the only scriptures known by Stephen, the first Christian martyr, were those recorded in the Old Testament. Paul, the greatest of all the great witnesses produced in the development of the kingdom, quoted freely from those old scrolls. These were the Scriptures, too, which Christ had absorbed and from which He gleaned divine comfort for His task. The wayside markings pointed like arrows to Golgotha. Whether we look forward or backward the cross is always the same. It is an eternal creation. Far back into the reaches of eternity it goes and springs from the heart of God when "the earth was waste and void and darkness was upon the face of the deep." But it makes us look forward as much, to the never ending joy and rapture of which the Book of Revelation speaks. The corridors of heaven shall some day resound as the ransomed hosts of God sing their praise to the "Lamb slain upon the cross."

But the cross is more than an eternal fact. It could be that, and yet do nothing for us, or it could destroy us. But "it is a faithful saying that Christ Jesus came into the world to save sinners," and it is an equally faithful saying that Jesus saves sinners by the cross. It is a saving fact, and without it no man could be rescued. That is why the cross is given such pre-eminence. When we speak of the cross, we mean the suffering and death of Jesus as expressed in the Gospels. Not all of the Gospels tell the story of His birth—only Luke does. Neither do all the Evangelists tell us about the temptation of Christ or His transfiguration or His ascension, but all with a united voice proclaim His death. That represents the outstanding fact of His Messianic ministry.

That we should hear so much about the death of Jesus has caused much questioning. Why not speak more about His life? It is true that we cannot speak too much about the life of one who was sin-free and pure, but it is equally true that we cannot understand life until we know how much Jesus was willing to sacrifice for our release and security. The example of Jesus would only reveal my impotence. It would only discourage me until I had stood in the shadow of the cross and felt its power sweep through my heart. The cross has a strange lifting power. It is the power of God unto salvation.

The cross gives us a better understanding of God—it gives us a new conception. Before Christ came, mankind was groping after God, more or less in the dark. Surely without the cross man could never have learned to know Him as a loving Father. The light streaming from Calvary reveals to us the completeness of divine understanding, the intensity of divine commiseration. It was no after-thought with God that He concluded to "heal grief with grief." God is not eager to punish. Calvary reveals His eagerness to atone and save.

Yes, there are eternal mysteries involved, but the saving fact of the cross is not beyond understanding. The New Testament has one great understandable explanation of the death of Christ. This is what the Word of God teaches: "Christ died for our sins." It marks the fulfillment of a divine plan. Men persecuted Him, the Romans actually crucified Him—but back of all this seeming tragedy is the counsel and plan of God. We must learn to see in the crucifixion, not only the evil perpetrated against Christ by His enemies—but the good which God, through the death of Christ, was able to accomplish for the race.

The thing in God which made the cross necessary was His justice and righteousness. The thing in man which made it necessary was sin. "How could God destroy sin without destroying the sinner?" God solved that problem as only God could. He permitted Christ to take our place, to become our substitute, and to bear our sins and their penalty. "He bare our sins in his own body on the tree." When that satisfaction was made, God could remit all penalties. On the night in which Jesus was betrayed He said to the disciples, as He instituted the Holy Sacrament of the Lord's Supper, "This cup is the New Testament in my blood which was shed for you and for many for the remission of sins." That was saying clearly, "My death makes your pardon possible."

> There was none other good enough
> To pay the price of sin,
> He only could unlock the gate
> Of heaven, and let us in.

Christ is my hope and only hope. When we say that we believe in the Lord Jesus Christ it means

that we trust Him and His merits with infinite
confidence. We take our refuge in Him and in
what He did for us upon the cross.

The devil confronted Luther in a dream. He
stood before him with an open book where all of
Luther's sins were entered. One by one the devil
reviewed these sins, and Luther was terrified until he suddenly remembered his faith in Christ.
Then he said to the devil: Those are my sins all
right, and black they are—your record of my sins
is correct. But there is one record you have forgotten. This is what you have forgotten: "The blood
of Jesus Christ cleanseth us from all sin."

The cross takes care of the penalty of sin, and
it also breaks the power of sin. No one can stand
in the presence of the cross and say, "I believe in
the Lord Jesus Christ," and then go out and love
to do that which is evil. The Christian, whether
he is strong or weak, will hate sin as much as he
hates the devil, the source and beginning of all
sin. The best preventive against sin and temptation is to take your station near the cross.

> Near the cross! O Lamb of God,
> Bring its scenes before me,
> Help me walk from day to day
> With its shadows o'er me.

A Strange Likeness

*All we like sheep have gone astray; we have turned every
one to his own way; and the* Lord *hath laid on him the
iniquity of us all.*   Isaiah 53:6

YOU may know something about sheep—there
may even be something about sheep which
fascinates you. Have you ever lifted a lamb into
your arms and felt that rapid, fearful heartbeat as
its wooly body struggled to be released? Or have
you ever had a lamb that was your own, where
all fear was gone and it snuggled closely as you
held it? Of all the domestic animals it is the kind-
est, the most helpless, and what is more, the most
stupid. Helpless and stupid. That tells quite a
story. In our text the prophet Isaiah says that we
have gone astray—gone astray just as sheep do because they are ignorant. They stray away from the
flock because they do not know any better.

We are all included in that comparison. None
of us is any better than a sheep. Men may differ
from each other in the way they have strayed, or
the direction they have gone. But they are like
sheep anyway. Just let a man go where he pleases
and you have your sheep. That is just what sheep
do, unless some one keeps them together.

Not all men are tempted in the same way, but
all men are tempted. Satan prepares a temptation
that will fit the inclinations of each individual.
Because of the different backgrounds, environ-
ments, and contacts the forms of sin will vary, too.
One temptation may not affect you, while it may
ruin and destroy another. The devil finds some
snare which in a peculiar way will touch you. His
presence bodes no good for anyone. Some people
are sensuous, selfish and vainglorious; the devil
knows just that. He probes and he feels his way
and when he finds the weak spot he attacks. Men
have built fine defences—Maginot lines—only to
have them outflanked by the enemy which storms
the citadel upon which they trusted so completely.

As we look back upon our past we are humbled,
and we penitently confess our sins before God.
Our personal transgressions have been many and
our wilfulness has grieved our Father in heaven.
We need to walk circumspectly because our na-
tures and our aptitudes will invite trouble. Let us
remember that we can be wrong in a thousand

ways, but there is only one way in which we can be right. Innumerable are the paths that lead to destruction, but only one way leads to God. We need to stop, look, and listen often to get our bearings and make sure that we are upon the right way. A careful and prayerful Lenten observance helps us to do just that.

Not all men are equally sinful, but all by nature have strayed. Ten thousand are the paths discovered by our lamentable ingenuity—paths that lead away from our Shepherd and King. And if our neighbor has sinned more often or more flagrantly than we have, let us not falsely imagine that there is no need for alarm. We may be overrating the sins of another while we are inclined to underrate our own. According to Isaiah, that apparent difference does not mean much, for "we have all gone astray." By nature man is sinful, and the mercy of God alone can save him. That is the force behind the Lenten call—"God, be merciful to me."

Ignorance and inherent foolishness cause men to stray from God, but the most tragic portion of the whole story is this, that when man discovers his error he is so helpless that he never can find his way back.

We have heard stories about wild cats and wild horses, wild cows and wild dogs, but never a story about wild sheep. Domestic animals, if left apart from the influence of men, will revert to type, some very readily and quickly. But the sheep is so helpless and defenseless that it can not last long enough outside the fold to revert to type. It will perish on the way. Never does a sheep sense danger until it is too late. It has no sense of direction and in this respect differs from the birds and animals with homing instincts that may guide them for hundreds of miles over trackless ways. Man, too, does not sense danger before it is too late. Man has no sense of direction. When he strays he cannot find his way back. The picture and the simile are still good.

A sheep may perish from hunger a few hundred feet from the most luscious pasturage and may die for want of water to drink when the fresh gurgling spring sparkles near by. The same sheep that strayed today may be gone again tomorrow. A lamb that wanders into the wilderness today, only to be searched for and found by the shepherd who fondles it and carries it home in his bosom, will make the same mistake again tomorrow. Spurgeon says of sheep that "they are Argus-eyed when it comes to finding the only break in the fence but blind as bats when it comes to finding the way home." The picture and the simile still hold. Man is that way, too.

But sheep never go astray intentionally. They do not mean to get lost; they are just true to na-

ture. They are stupid, exceedingly stupid. They
can become so absorbed in eating grass that they
nibble and nibble until they have strayed from
the flock. That is what man does. Thoughtlessly,
he gets his head down in devoting himself to making money, to enlarging his barns, to increasing
his wealth—almost imperceptibly at times, it seems,
but he loses the flock. He strays from the fold into
worldliness and is destroyed. Man gets his head
down to enjoy the pleasures of the moment, for
they thrill and fascinate; but when his eyes lift
again, the shepherd and the fold are gone.

That is why Isaiah says, "We all like sheep have
gone astray." The characterization is still humil-
iating, but the prophet does not leave us there,
hopeless, helpless, and hapless though we may be.
The same prophet brings words of comfort and
consolation. In spite of the fact that stupidity and
helplessness are classed with iniquity, there is still
hope. This is what Isaiah says: "The Lord hath
laid on him the iniquity of us all." God found a
way again. We can not be so hopeless nor so helpless, but that God can do something for us.

What a heap of iniquity we have gathered because we are foolish. We have sinned with our
hands, our eyes, our ears, our hearts; we have
sinned against the Word of God and done violence
to our own conscience. From Adam's fall to the
end of time it will be so. But "God laid on him

the iniquity of us all." The Servant of God absorbed the blows that should have fallen upon us. The burden of all sins, individual and collective, was laid on Him. When we are called to account for our own individual sins, "we cannot answer one in a thousand." How great, then, is the burden of all men's sin. When the Servant of God took the place of sinners, the weight of that load was immeasurable. In the scales of divine justice it must have been equivalent to the punishment due the whole race for all its sins. The lash of punishment smote Him. That which had been scattered abroad was centered upon Jesus in fearful concentration.

Do you wonder then why He prayed in Gethsemane, "Lord, remove this cup from me, if it be possible"? The consequences of sin are too awful to contemplate, not to say endure. Do you think it strange that He was prostrated during that lonely vigil in the garden when "his sweat was as it were great drops of blood"? Death, which is the final and ultimate accounting for sin, must be faced by Him. Thus the Son of God became a curse, for us.

We know the story of His crucifixion, but the height, the length, the breadth, and the depth of His agony no man will ever understand. Angels might have understood, but the tongue of man could never adequately describe the passion which mutilated the heart of Jesus.

The torture of the cross certainly did not cause His greatest pain. He was prepared for that because He knew that He would "be lifted up," but He also knew that there would be a speedy resurrection to glory. The mysterious agony of soul was caused by something far more terrifying. Martyrs faced death bravely without a trace of fear in after years. They endured with joy and rapture.

The agony that beset Him was caused by His conflict with the adversary, from whose tyrannizing power He came to set us free. Satan desired to set at naught, by any means, the counsels of God. This was particularly the devil's hour, and he did his best. Even then we cannot fully understand the sorrowful apprehension which overwhelmed His soul. He was alone — the heavens were closed against Him. Alone on the cross, the bearer of our iniquity, and God would not and could not hear Him. The inevitable terrorized Him.

"It pleased God to bruise him." That does not mean that God was glad Jesus was suffering. God permitted Him so to suffer in order that we might be spared. The cross was a mysterious infliction by God upon one who was innocent; "the Lamb of God that taketh away the sin of the world" was upon the altar of sacrifice. He bore the sins of many, yours and mine were included, too—and He sank, crushed beneath the load. May we say that, in some sense, the poison and the bitterness of sin entered into His soul? He had all the appearances of a sinner, punished for enormous guilt.

> Go to dark Gethsemane,
> Ye that feel the tempter's power;
> Your Redeemer's conflict see,
> Watch with Him one bitter hour;
> Turn not from His grief away,
> Learn of Jesus Christ to pray.
>
> Calvary's mournful mountain climb,
> There, adoring at His feet,
> Mark that miracle of time,
> God's own sacrifice complete;
> "It is finished," hear the cry,
> Learn of Jesus Christ to die.

Never was Jesus more perfect or more acceptable unto God, than when upon the cross in lonely anguish He cried, "Eli, Eli, lama sabachthani." Because of our sins the divine comforting assurance was withdrawn, but now Jesus did not waver. How the angels in heaven must have watched and waited, interceding for victory; and how the heavens must have resounded with joy when Jesus said, "It it finished," and God again could say, as He so often had said before, "This is my beloved Son in whom I am well pleased."

Beautiful Savior, King of creation,
Son of God and Son of man,
Truly I'd love Thee, truly I'd serve Thee,
Light of my soul, my joy, my crown.

The Day Is Triumphant

*And when the sabbath was past, Mary Magdalene, and
Mary the mother of James, and Salome, had bought sweet
spices, that they might come and anoint him. And very
early in the morning the first day of the week, they came
unto the sepulchre at the rising of the sun. And they said
among themselves, Who shall roll us away the stone from
the door of the sepulchre? And when they looked, they
saw that the stone was rolled away: for it was very great.
And entering into the sepulchre, they saw a young man
sitting on the right side, clothed in a long white garment;
and they were affrighted. And he saith unto them, Be not
affrighted: Ye seek Jesus of Nazareth, which was crucified: he is risen; he is not here: behold the place where
they laid him. But go your way, tell his disciples and
Peter that he goeth before you into Galilee: there shall
ye see him, as he said unto you.*   Mark 16:1-7

IN God's entire economy there is no other day
like Easter Day. It is a day of hopes made real
and of dreams come true. The Easter songs are

songs of praise, and the notes of assured victory
are clear as bells that ring. From the Atlantic to
the Pacific, from Australia to Europe, from fox
holes and slit trenches, from army camps and
training centers, from battleships and battlefields
has rung today the glad refrain, "He is arisen."

Over Golgotha darkness had hung like a mantle
—and how long that night seemed; in Joseph's
rock-hewn grave Jesus lay; Judas had gone the
way of the world, a victim of despair; Peter with
scalding tears had penitently acknowledged un-
faithfulness to his Master and friend; the disciples
were scattered like shepherdless sheep, for their
hopes like the Master lay buried in a tomb that
was sealed; Roman soldiers alone, with clanking
swords, broke the silence of death which brooded
over the grave.

The Son of God lay dead in the tomb. Out from
the dens of evil rang the shouts of victory; evil
would enjoy the fruits of her labor unmolested,
so they thought. The disciples wept because their
Lord and Master had suffered so, and now He was
no more. But "God moves in a mysterious way His
wonders to perform." Soon the foes were disillu-
sioned, and the joy of the world was changed to
sorrow and fear. Soon the sorrow of helpless, weeping friends was transformed into ecstatic, speechless joy. It was the Psalmist who said, "Weeping
may endure for a night, but joy cometh in the

morning." Jesus the crucified one is arisen, death
is swallowed up in victory. That is the Easter message today. It is old but ever new.

For nineteen hundred years unbelief has tried
to discredit the resurrection story, to set at nought
the angel's proclamation, "He is arisen." That the
enemies have miserably failed is evidenced by the
millions who today sing their praises of a risen
Lord. The veracity of the gospel story has never
been shaken. Easter is the joyous sequel which follows the tragic events which occurred on Good
Friday. Without that sequel the cross episode
would have been a useless tragedy that marked
the course of a fallen race. And many are the
tragedies that cannot be explained or yet be con-
doned.

The climax of the career of Jesus of Nazareth
came not on Calvary's hill, but it occurred in
Joseph's garden on Easter morning when, in the
words of the Apostle Paul, "He was declared to be
the Son of God with power by the resurrection
from the dead." The blasphemy of the scribes, the
chief priests and the elders was thereby answered.
You recall how they taunted Him as He hung
upon the cross, saying, "He trusted in God, let
him deliver him now, if he will have him, for he
said, I am the Son of God." God did approve Him
as His Son and forever stamped His approval upon
every word He spoke and upon every deed He

wrought. So long as the world stands He shall not
want faithful servants who will lay down their lives
if need be to preach the resurrection. God help me
if I do not preach that He died according to the
Scriptures and that according to the same Scriptures He rose again. That is my mandate. The ob-
jection of the world cannot silence the preaching
of the resurrection; neither can enmity, hatred,
and persecution stifle the voice of praise in the
heart of a grateful humanity. Witnesses have come
"as dew out of the bosom of the morning," to
preach a living Christ. Martin Luther inscribed
upon his table and upon the walls of his room,
"Vivit, vivit": He lives, He lives. Peter on Pentecost day proclaimed the same message, and thousands repented and believed. The Apostle Paul
preached the resurrection in all the ancient cul-
tural centers until the kingdom flourished and the
name of Christ was honored. Millions have since
relayed the message until men the world over have
heard. Martinson, one of our distinguished missionaries in China, as he lay dying, flung his arms
heavenward saying, "He has conquered and I have
conquered."

I know that Christ lives because He lives in me.
A faith such as that cannot put us to shame. We
place our hands upon our hearts and we say, I
know He lives because He is there. Christ lives in
me because He guides and rules my thoughts, my

words, my deeds, and He gives me strength to
take up the cross and and follow Him.

What would your baptism be, and your confir-
mation, your church membership, if He were a
dead Savior? You would be confessing a lie, I
would be preaching a lie, and the congregation
would be believing a lie. We would all have a part
in the greatest ecclesiastical hoax ever perpetrated
upon man.

The world has changed much in these nineteen
hundred years. Many things have been outgrown.
But the fixed, solid, unmovable bulwark and citadel of our salvation, which is the resurrection of
Christ from the dead, has not changed. Human
hands can distort but not destroy a fact. Stand face
to face with your conscience, look at the multitude
of your sins and the damning sentence of the law,
and you will know what Paul meant with his
triumphant assertion, "Christ is risen from the
dead." Look into the dark sepulchral chamber
that swallows a loved one and you will know what
the resurrection means.

The joy you find in the resurrection will be
commensurate with the knowledge of your needs.
When you think of your sins, look into the opened
and empty sepulchre and learn to say confidently,
"Thanks be to God who giveth us the victory
through our Lord Jesus Christ." Death, where is
thy sting, and grave thy victory?

There were men in Paul's time, too, who said that Jesus had not arisen from the dead, but he argued that there was no use in accepting Christ at all if you eliminate the resurrection. If Jesus remained in the grave then we are yet in our sins. The price and the penalty of sin has not been paid and approved. Then the faith of all the saints who have gone before us is vain. The logic Paul employs is this: "Now is Christ risen from the dead," and just as He was raised from the dead, becoming the first fruits of them that sleep, so shall we also be raised from the dead.

Most of us have celebrated many Easters. We have heard the old story about the resurrection of Christ so often that we have come to take it for granted. "The inaudible and noiseless foot of time moves with rapid pace." It is very probable that some of us shall not hear the Easter proclamation repeated very many times more. "Our hearts like muffled drums are beating funeral marches to the grave."

Has the Easter message we have so often heard really made much difference in our living? There is an inevitable drift of things in life. We are fluid, not static. Either life as it progresses becomes very pregnant with meaningful things, or by the same token it becomes more and more empty and meaningless. Life can be poor, or it can be rich. These tendencies are universal. The steady rhythmic beats of time produce within us either life or death. Life and death eternal are present, not post mortem, possessions. Immortality is a quality which every man possesses. Immortality may be good or it may be bad, depending upon whether we choose to be with God or away from God. Eternal death is always away from God. Either we are immortally with God or we are immortally away from God. But who would honestly care for an existence after death if it must be apart from God? Eternal life begins here and now. The disciples who walked with Jesus came to possess it, and the faithful ones of every age have learned to know its gracious meaning, its precious value. It was the Savior who by His resurrection "brought life and immortality to light."

Most of us are called upon to face approximately the same experiences. It may be good fortune or bad fortune, success or failure, trouble or triumph, health or sickness. Nearly everything happens to everyone. But the subsequent emotional reactions will differ as much as night and day. The difference lies in the interpretation and application.

"We are born to trouble as the sparks fly upward." That is what Job said, and he certainly knew. In the face of all the adversity thrust upon him he could say, "The Lord gave, the Lord hath taken away, blessed be the name of the Lord." With Paul he could also have said, "All things

work together for good to them that love God."
Blessed are they who can say, "The sufferings of
the present time are not worthy to be compared to
the glory which shall be revealed." That is one
interpretation, that the ills are beneficial. Another
person facing the same trials will take issue with
the Creator and say, "It must be an ill advised
God who permits so many things to happen." That
is the philosophy of unbelief. We pray God to deliver us from such empty thinking.

How much we desire that Easter and its glad
message shall constitute our key to happiness! The
restless race is seeking for happiness. Men may
vary in external things: they may be rich or poor,
high or low, intelligent or ignorant; but their aims
are the same and their aspirations are alike: give
us happiness; make our hearts glad.

We would like to tell all the world: "Come
with us and we will do you good." Some would
understand and others would not. There are those
who feel that the church would make them sad
instead of glad. We shall have to admit that during the past week we have been daily near the
cross and that the symbol of Christianity is the
cross. Even our churches are builded cruciform.
They would say to us that we are unreasonable
to expect them to be happy with the cross for a
shelter. And it must be admitted that Christianity has a sobering influence. It made Paul's life

sober, but it did something for him. When he sailed the seas where Anthony and Cleopatra had floated their gilded barges it was because he wished to share his joys with all people. He was sober, but of all men most joyous. The Christian life is no fairy land, and the record of Christianity is one of conflict with the powers of darkness. The way of the kingdom is not strewn with roses, and those who walk therein will have to grapple with the grim and "dirty facts" of life.

The world in its search for happiness goes from one extremity to another. More is always needed to satisfy, and when men sense they are slipping or losing their hold they only hold tighter and quicken their pace. Then one day a crash comes. Maybe it is insanity, maybe it is despair. At any rate, they "sink to the level of modern disillusionment," and the issue is cynicism. Then follows the utter abandonment of all principle and all hope. But the church of the resurrection cries out to a world in despair: "Pull yourself together, Christ is arisen from the dead. Keep one hand on time and the other on eternity."

When life loses its meaning, stand at the cross for a while. Watch prayerfully the things that happen there—then pause for a few minutes to view the empty sepulchre and to hear the angel say, "He is arisen; he is not here." Then the acme of joy will thrill you.

I know that my Redeemer lives!
What comfort this sweet sentence gives!
He lives, He lives who once was dead,
He lives my ever-living Head.

He lives, all glory to His name,
He lives my Jesus still the same;
Oh, the sweet joy this sentence gives,
I know that my Redeemer lives.

That is the victory song of a ransomed soul come
into his own. The quality of that experience is
rich and radiant. Life becomes different—so rich,
so full and free. "Old things are passed away, behold, all things are become new."

When Easter sings across the world,
I think that every sea
Reflects the blue that danced upon
The waves of Galilee.
I like to think that kinder words
To weary folks are said,
Because Christ toiled up Calvary,
With tired down-bent head.

Prepared
for the Conflict

*Rejoicing in hope; patient in tribulation; continuing
instant in prayer.*   Romans 12:12

ANOTHER year has hurried by and we have
come to another Lent. The season of Lent
has become a resting place for souls that are weary.
Lengthening days provide more sunshine and
warmth for bodies that are languid; and thirsting
souls are satisfied and refreshed as they drink of
the living waters. The heart is filled with a
strange longing for home and heaven, where the
tools of labor shall be laid aside and rest shall be
eternal. That yearning for rest and home will some
day be fully satisfied. That will be at the end of
the way—when we reach the terminus, the goal of
all our efforts, the hope of every aspiration.

When Lent comes we are asked to pause before the cross—to look and learn. The cross and the Christ will unfold for us there a redemption that will make our burdens seem small and of little consequence. Since God gave His only begotten Son to be a sin-offering for us, is there anything good that He would withhold from us? His love and His patience are overwhelming. As we observe the scene enacted on Calvary we begin to understand a little better that "God is love." When we see the wearied Master hanging there, our feeling of weariness is gone and we arise strengthened for our task. There is much to be done—and the time is short; there is truth to be defended—and the enemy is strong. The circumstances are grim and the occasion calls for men who are faithful and strong.

Jesus needed to be prepared for His conflict with the powers of darkness. The Gethsemane rendezvous made Him strong for the Calvary scenes that lay so close by. An angel came ministering comfort and the strength He needed. Thus He was enabled to enter the holy of holies once for all. He was prepared to face Annas and Caiaphas, Pilate and the mob. He bore His pain and His anguish silently as a lamb that is led to the slaughter. Never once did He waver in His purpose after He left the garden; and when the painful hours closed upon the scene, a voice from the cross came out of the darkness—"It is finished"—and songs of joy and victory must have rung through the heavens when the celestial hosts observed what had transpired.

The angels of God are girding men for victory today—helping us to share in the victory which He won for us. Lent is meant to be helpful. Its purpose is to ease the burden—not to increase it; to take away the restless spirit and to give us peace instead; to create within us a spirit of joy consonant with our faith. If our task seems to be heavy and oppressive it will yield more readily to a singing, victorious faith.

The Apostle Paul was prepared for his conflicts. He more than any other man knew life at its best and at its worst. What had been accomplished within his heart, he knew could be accomplished within the hearts of others; what had been done for him could in turn be done for others.

In this letter to the Roman congregation, he counsels his friends there, "Rejoicing in hope, patient in tribulation, continuing stedfastly in prayer." The times would change for them. He foresaw the most bitter hatreds and persecutions. It would be hard for his friends then, but they must be hopeful, patient, and prayerful; and how could they be, unless they were first prepared and strengthened for the conflict.

I have heard many unkind words spoken about

the effect of Christianity. It has been called a sorrowful religion. Yes, there is a place for sorrow, but there is also a place for infinite joy. Christianity has been called a bitter wind which blights and withers every flower. That this was not the kind of Christianity which captivated and motivated Paul is very evident. "Rejoice—rejoice—and again I say rejoice." That is Paul's refrain. His buoyant spirit never sags, though he faces the Sanhedrin or Agrippa or Festus or the headsman. The sky above him is always clear.

Paul was not moved by any superficial, apostolic optimism. He was a good observer; he was a good thinker, unprejudiced in his judgments. He knew what was in man, and he was familiar with the degradations wrought by sin. Read Romans One, and you will find out what he knew. It is from the evils envisaged there that the clean, optimistic words of our text emerge. How was it possible for Paul to rejoice in the face of so much that was evil? First, he fixed his eyes upon the redemption of Christ. He lived and labored in an atmosphere of redemption. Redemption was the spirit of his life—it kept him going when the way was hard. He said to himself, "He has redeemed me. I am bought with a great price. I belong to Him." To Paul that was a great deliverance. He rejoiced when he thought of the things yet to be revealed. "I shall live and reign with Him in all eternity."

With such a prospect he could be hopeful. He thought of the unlimited resources placed at his disposal. He already had great possessions and he was promised even more. Militant personality that he was, he dashed the tears of apprehension from his cheeks and marched triumphantly on with a victorious faith that was joyous. "I can do all things through Christ who strengtheneth me." He fixed his heart upon glory yet to be revealed. He might have lost himself in the pain of the moment, but he did not. There may have been periods in the development of the kingdom of God when men have been too imbued with the spirit of "other-worldliness," but that kind of thinking is largely absent in our modern religious life. There may have been occasions when men have devoted so much time to the things that are to be, that they have neglected present duties. Certainly that criticism does not hold today, and I believe we have lost immeasurably by uprooting that contemplative spirit. Certain it is that our personality, cleansed and glorified, will find a new and better expression there. There is much to think about on the other side. A little more of that thinking might check the materialistic views so apparent today.

What a hope lies, too, in the fact that we shall recover lost friends there; dear ones shall be restored to us. Is it all over when they go from us here? The heart refuses to believe that and clings to the thought of reunion. We shall find them there, the young and the aged, soldiers and civilians. It was John who said, "And their works do follow them." The remuneration is often scant here, and we often feel that our accomplishments are meager. We try to do a few things but nothing much comes of it. There we shall see all things again in a different light, and every kindly thought or word or deed shall add joy to our salvation. I wish I could do much for a Savior who has been so generous with me. Others there will be, too, who shall share the joy with us. There is much in the other world to make me glad. It is a real hope, and Paul calls it a living hope.

He also urges the Roman Christians to be patient in tribulation. Paul left his people a good example. His life was in peril on numerous occasions, but he always retained a quiet composure. Wicked men withstood him on every hand, yet he was patient. He had to fight disturbances in his churches—vile sins sometimes, evil doctrines introduced by his enemies—but knowing the ultimate victory he was patient. In every tribulation, whether he "passively suffered or actively endured," he was patient. We must be sure, however, that our troubles and tribulations are not self made. Men do sometimes make their own sorrows. They have troubles, but they lie largely in the

imagination. As Christians we cannot invite tribulation by indiscretion. That has been done, too.

Some tribulations come from without, that is,
actual suffering caused by others. Paul probably
had that in mind when he asked them to be patient.
There were dark foreboding clouds; persecutions
were coming and they must be prepared for that
eventuality. Nero, hardened in vice, must find
someone upon whom he could wreak vengeance
and upon whom he could charge his sin.

Tribulations rise from within; most often that
is where they are found. Paul's thorn in the flesh
may have caused him much trouble. There are
mental and spiritual struggles with which every
Christian must contend: doubts, fears, anxieties,
failures, ingratitude. Be patient still. Victory will
ultimately be yours if you are faithful.

A Christian who had no vehicle by which to
reach God would be ill prepared for any conflict.
Prayer is such a vehicle. To pray is to draw near
to God, to lose yourself in His infinite grace. How
near God sometimes has been when we have talked
with Him in prayer! Paul was afraid their efforts
might be relaxed. They must be prepared to pray
more than ever.

Let us make our Lenten observance a season of
persistent prayer. Prayers are answered, but many
are not granted. If God's will is done, all is well.

A Man of Sorrows

He is despised and rejected of men; a man of sorrows, and acquainted with grief: and we hid as it were our faces from him; he was despised, and we esteemed him not. Isaiah 53:3

ISAIAH, gifted and imbued with the clear vision of an ancient seer, anticipates in this chapter the facts recorded eight or nine hundred years later by Matthew, Mark, Luke, and John. What he foretold came to pass. Even a cursory reading of the New Testament story substantiates that Christ, when He came, "was despised and rejected of men, a man of sorrows and acquainted with grief."

Isaiah recognized that the Servant of the Lord would be held in contempt—that men would be held from him by a strange aversion. "As one from whom men hide their faces he was despised and we esteemed him not." At His coming, men turned from Him. They did not recognize Him for it is written, "They knew him not." Nor did they wish to look upon Him. They simply did not care.

As the root of all sin is to be found in unbelief, so unbelief was the cause for the rejection. Isaiah asks in the first verse of this chapter, "Who hath believed our report?" and the Apostle Paul says, "God hath concluded them all in unbelief." God had revealed much through other prophets, too, but the people did not understand. They looked upon the prophets as a necessary institution and longed for them when the prophetic voice was silenced, and yet they discredited the teachings and visions of these men of God. There were times when it was convenient for them to hear the prophets, and there were times when they refused to hear. Sometimes the people recognized the voice of God when the prophet spoke, and sometimes they wounded them brutally or killed them, all because of unbelief. From the earliest prophecy in Genesis where Christ is called the "seed of the woman," to Malachi, where He is called the "sun of righteousness," they could read of His greatness. But they would neither accept Him nor believe in Him. Then God silenced the prophetic voice for four hundred years. From Malachi to John the Baptist not a voice was heard.

The divine oracle was strangely silent. For many

years they waited and wondered and longed for the familiar voice. The scribes bent studiously over the ancient scrolls, seeking to discern the time and place and manner of the Messiah's coming. To them it seemed they were a forsaken people, that God was far away. When they failed to receive any new revelation they had to make the best of what they had.

Then one day, out in the wilderness, they heard the voice of God once more. They listened, they were inspired, many of them repented, confessing their sins, and were baptized by John in the Jordan. They asked him who he was. "Only a voice in the wilderness," was his reply. But it was the voice of a prophet and to them the voice of God. They accepted him until he committed his disciples and friends to the "Lamb of God who taketh away the sin of the world." Then they believed no more, and John was executed by Herod and the plans were laid for the execution of Jesus, too, while the voice of John still echoed in the Judean hills.

The whole economy—so they thought—was unreasonable and not acceptable. They were disappointed in His humble parentage and appearance. Here is one, the child of a lowly virgin, called the son of a carpenter in Nazareth, who claims to be the royal heir to the throne of His father David. Ridiculous! This man had lived in obscurity for thirty years, toiling over a carpenter's bench; He was poor and later had no home of His own, no place to lay His head. He had a few friends, but who were they? Just fishermen from Galilee who made their humble living with a fishing smack as they plied the stormy waters of Tiberias. Jesus, without any ecclesiastical authority, went about from place to place as an itinerant preacher and teacher. He looked like "a root out of dry ground." Surely there was not much to commend Him, and they reasoned that He was not the Christ. How could He be, if their Messianic interpretations were correct? So they despised Him, and because they despised Him they also rejected Him.

The Jews were ashamed to own Him because of the way He lived. Notwithstanding the wisdom and the grace of His words, the extraordinary power of His miracles, and the "unapproachable beauty of His character," they found in Him "no form nor comeliness." The proud Pharisees and the skeptical Sadducees could not bear Him. Finally, to eliminate Him, they slandered and accused Him falsely, convicted Him before Pilate's tribunal, and the servants of Rome crucified Him as a deceiver and impostor.

It is not so hard to understand that some could hate Him—that even many hated Him—for truth and justice will always be hated by unrighteousness. The ecclesiastics of His time who believed that true religion consisted in outward observances were naturally angered when He told them that these things availed nothing, that they were spending their time on useless non-essentials. Yes, they could hate Him, but how could they despise one so kind and true and pure and beneficent? But such was the case from the high priest down, and they wanted to forget Him.

In one of the commentaries on this particular portion of Scripture, a story by Anatole France is retold. Pilate is represented as conversing with an old friend about bygone days. They are talking about the Jewish women, and special reference is made to Mary Magdalene whom both had known. The friend remarks about the strange things that happened to her when she left him to join the young miracle worker who had come from Nazareth in Galilee. His name was Jesus and they crucified Him for some reason or other. "Pontius, do you remember the man?" The old procurator frowned and raised a hand to his forehead as if he were trying hard to recall. After a moment of silence he said, "Did you say Jesus—Jesus of Nazareth? No, I don't remember him." Do you think Pilate could ever forget? He could despise and hate and reject, but he never could forget the awful crucifixion scenes on Calvary that black Friday while Jesus hung on the cross, when the elements trembled and were confused, and everything seemed to go black, as though nature shuddered at the scene while the sun hid its face altogether and darkness prevailed for hours. The historic annals recorded these strange phenomena lest even Pilate should forget, not to mention the cursing mob which had screamed for His crucifixion.

Pilate tried to wash his hands of all responsibility—but responsibility, like Banquo's ghost, kept coming back, and Pilate, according to tradition, was drowned in the same despair as Judas was. Those who despise and reject Christ, be they Jews or Gentiles, ultimately find that they are despised and neglected of God.

When hell let loose its inferno of sin and death, Jesus smashed it head-on, and in the impact He was bruised. It would be strange, indeed, if the faithful followers of Jesus would escape every wound. Peter, James, and John received many hurts in His name, and Paul was brutally treated for his faith in Jesus who was crucified.

Jesus was a man of sorrows. He was made up of sorrows. These were the constituent elements of His being. Sorrow was His peculiar token—the mark of identification which He bore. He might have been described by the ancient prophet as a man of holiness, for He was that. There was no sin in Him—He had no fault. He might have been called a man of labors; for His energies found ready expression in doing the Father's work. He

was active day and night, early and late, bearing
burdens, bringing comfort, supplying needs. He
might have been called a man of eloquence, for
He was that. "Never man spake like this man,"
they said. But He was a man of sorrows in a most
striking way. "His visage was marred more than
any man, and His form more than the sons of
men," by reason of the incessant burdens imposed
by sorrow.

He must have been very lonely, a stranger
among His own kinsmen, for those who loved
Him there knew Him not. Many times His heart
was full, but there was no one with whom He
could share His griefs. The disciples, while they
were faithful to Him, never really understood
Him until after Pentecost.

He was painfully sensitive to the sorrows endured by others, too. Everyone's sorrow belonged
to Him. His heart must inevitably hold much of
pain. The pains, the fears, the anxieties endured
by the degraded, neglected, and friendless, were
felt by Him. "In all their afflictions he was afflicted." He commiserated with all manner of men
and all types of suffering

Sin deserves sorrow, and we are in our element
of sorrow because we have sinned. But sin has a
way of deadening sorrow; it becomes more blunt
and less piercing. However, when Jesus entered
into sorrow He was altogether out of His element

because He had no sin. Our hands and our hearts
grow callous with repeated sins, but Jesus was
delicately sensitive to all that was wrong. Because
of our constant association with some forms of sin,
they become unrecognizable, but they all touched
Him deeply.

Perhaps the hypocrisy of His time caused His
chief concern. It met Him everywhere, especially
in the house of God. The life and vitality of religion among the leaders was utterly destroyed.
Pride, selfishness, long prayers to be heard of men,
lying, misinterpretation, and the evil eye—these
confronted Him at all times, everywhere. Then
there was Judas the traitor. Jesus knew from the
beginning that Judas would betray Him, yet He
permitted him to remain with the disciples. We
cannot possibly comprehend the divine forbear-
ance required.

The greatest sorrow overwhelmed Him when
"he who knew no sin was made to be sin for us."
He who was pure and undefiled, who had braved
every storm so courageously, was in the end "num-
bered with transgressors." "It pleased the Father
to bruise him, he hath put him to grief." We see
Him in the Garden of Gethsemane, bowed into
the dust, saying, "My soul is exceeding sorrowful,
even unto death." And we hear Him again when
pain and lonely sorrow wring this cry from His
lips on Calvary, "My God, my God, why hast

thou forsaken me?" He was bearing our sins then. He was making a way where there was no way, faithful to the uttermost, faithful until His task was finished. Truly His love was great, and for it I should love Him, too.

The Master did not fail in the crucial moment, though His physical energies were utterly spent. When those who murdered Him thought He was vanquished forever His kingdom really took root.

Behold the man! He grips me! He holds me with an irresistible hand. Despised and rejected He may be, but He shall be my King and my God.

The Chastisement of
Our Peace

Surely he hath borne our griefs, and carried our sorrows: yet we did esteem him stricken, smitten of God, and afflicted. But he was wounded for our transgressions, he was bruised for our iniquities: the chastisement of our peace was upon him; and with his stripes we are healed.

Isaiah 53:4-5

NOWHERE else in the Old Testament is the truth concerning the suffering Messiah brought out in such fulness. The prophet speaks as though he had been present during the trial and crucifixion of Jesus, so clearly does he discern the divine plans to be unfolded. The passage we have before us is often repeated in the New Testament. And rightly so, for this chapter in Isaiah is essentially evangelical, and we can take any verse and do as Philip did to the Ethiopian eunuch and preach Christ. The doctrines of the atonement and vicarious suffering are clearly anticipated. Into the fellowship of human suffering, Christ the sinless one is led as a lamb to the slaughter. Isaiah recognizes that "he was wounded for our transgressions and bruised for our iniquities." The episode on Calvary, cruel and brutal as it was, happened because of our need. Christ, the Lamb of God, was chastised to bring peace to a race doomed to sin and its sequel which is death.

Sin is an incurable disease. There would be no need to speak of healing if sin were not regarded by God as a disease. Sin is a trespass, a transgression, an iniquity, but it is also a sickness. Sin is in man's system and he cannot deny it or destroy it. He cannot even do as he wishes—the sickness makes him do wrong. If man were well he would not do and say the things which have made him guilty. There is a deep corruption and an evil inclination in his nature by birth, about which he can do nothing. The results precipitated by this disease he deals with just as helplessly. Something has entered his system from without which causes all these strange expressions. Man was not that way when God created him. Then he was perfect, there was nothing wrong. In soul, in spirit, in body he was well, and he represented the highest product of God's creative genius. The present sickness is an abnormality precipitated by the fall of our first parents. Since the day of the fall everyone has been tainted by this evil tendency. No one escapes. Every mother's son born into this world is afflicted. When man yielded to temptation something happened, not only to those who disobeyed God, but even to the unborn race which was doomed to suffer relentlessly. The poisoned dart called sin became embedded in the flesh and could be extracted only by the sovereign grace of God. So long as the dart remains the system will be poisoned and sick. Only God can remove sin and the dart that caused it, and the poison and sickness will linger long after the power of sin is broken. The time of convalescence is long and trying, and not until death comes will sin be wholly rooted out. It has done irreparable harm, and great scar tissues of wounds that are healed mark the soul.

Just as bodily disease upsets the whole system and reacts upon every physical function, so sin puts all our spiritual faculties out of commission. If one organ is sick all the other organs will eventually suffer with it. A sick man's system does not work right—one derangement causes others until there is a final fatal breakdown. So it is with sin in our system. It is reflected in all our thinking. Our will becomes powerless to do the good, our imagination is defiled, our conscience becomes less active—in fact the whole spiritual body is sick, and unless something is done to check the progress of the disease the spirit will be destroyed.

Sin is strangely paralyzing in its effect. Man becomes incapacitated for work, his appetite is gone, his rest is disturbed, and yet he is unable to do anything which might help. He cannot even will to do right. He is so utterly palsied that he cannot of his own strength even lay hold on the Savior; he is defenseless altogether against sin in every form; he is unable to pray and mourn his case before God. That is the tragic and pathetic consummation worked by sin in its finality. It is an utter, abject, lonely helplessness.

Sin is like a disease in that it either causes great pain or it succeeds in deadening all sensibility. Sin in its beginning brings sorrow and remorse—little else. But when the pain is gone the deadly work is completed. Maybe we can understand why David pleaded, "Take not thy Holy Spirit from me." Take anything else—my will, my reason, my imagination, but please, God, do not take away the voice of conscience. We can manage without a lot of things if they are taken from us, but we cannot find the way if the voice within ceases to prompt.

Home remedies will not avail against anything as serious as sin. You will do well to call the Great Physician. Help must come from without, resident forces are inadequate. Let us not be deceived, "The wages of sin is death."

Nature is a wonderful healer. Nature takes care of many illnesses. Nature will heal a bruise or a cut or a broken bone—a wonderful agent to repair injuries so well. But nature cannot heal the wounds inflicted by sin. There is no natural recovery. Generally things go from bad to worse. Social traditions and restrictions may slow the downward tendency, but the malady issues at last in spiritual and eternal death.

Is there no way then to assure recovery and healing for a sin-sick soul? Yes, there is. What man cannot do, God can. Where there is no way God makes a way and helps the race and still maintains His integral justice. But the help must be extended from without and be administered by a power that is stronger. This is the vicarious healing of which the Scriptures speak. "By his stripes we are healed."

When we speak of the vicarious atonement we mean the atonement brought about by Christ's suffering for man, when He assumed the guilt and punishment justly due us for our sins. Until that atonement was consummated, neither the power of sin could be broken nor the punishment for sin averted. Then alone could the universal contagion called sin be healed.

The great Sin-Bearer must be a voluntary victim laying down His life freely. He must be a spotless victim, for one spot or taint would destroy the efficacy of the sacrifice He volunteered to make. It must be a sinless one for the sinful. He must be able to make satisfaction for the sins of the whole world. Man could not do that—the blood of his sacrifice could not be of infinite value. To do a thing which would affect and benefit all, those returned to dust and those not yet formed, would require a power equivalent to that possessed by the Creator and Preserver of the universe. But to enter into our walk, to endure our pain, to bear our burdens and to share our sufferings, this Servant of the Lord must be clothed in flesh. He must be cast in our mould. Deep and dark is the mystery surrounding the Lamb of God upon the altar of sacrifice. Incomprehensible it may be to us, but the Scriptures which are the Word of God—and we have no further revelation — plainly teach, "Christ died for our sins." In the economy of God He enters as our Substitute. He volunteers to bear our sins for us and to take upon Himself our guilt. That means He would have to die for us, and He knew it. That makes His love great.

I pause for a moment to watch the humbled Savior carrying His cross over the narrow, tortuous Via Dolorosa; the clouds are black and hanging low. We see Him reviled by the executioners and mocked by the mob that accompanies Him to Calvary, called skull hill. There they crucify Him and God inaugurates the first blackout as we catch the dying cry, "It is finished." Through blinding, commiserating lines we read again, "He was wounded for our transgressions and bruised for our iniquities. The chastisement of our peace was upon him and with his stripes we are healed." O God, take the dimness from my eyes and let me see. I want to see Him dying there. Then help me never to forget. It was for me!

The vicarious principle of sacrifice is asserted by the Word of God, though we may not be able to explain it—certainly we cannot prove it to an unbelieving world. And yet that principle prevails in the lower kingdoms. The mineral kingdom gives itself for the vegetable, and the vegetable gives itself for the animal. The principle is illustrated in the mother who gives of herself cheerfully in order that the children may benefit. She wears herself out, dying often at an early age because she gave all to help those she loved. In fact, it represents the very constitution of the physical world. God's providential plans included it.

Why should it be so difficult to believe that our guilt can be transferred to another? Was God unjust in permitting Christ to suffer for us? If a friend pays our debt for us, is the creditor unjust who accepts the payment, so long as it was voluntarily made? The principle is not at variance with the nature of God, else it would not prevail in every sphere. We let it alone; it is God's place.

The words He has spoken are, Yea and Amen. Mystery of mysteries, "We see through a glass darkly."

Even in the intellectual being the vicarious principle obtains. Every thought which we absorb is the fruit of another's wearisome vigilance. The civilization we now enjoy is the product of the millions who have labored and died for us. The principles obtaining in our democratic form of government are the fruit of vicarious suffering upon the battlefields and on our frontiers as workmen wielded their skill. We are standing upon a scaffold which they builded for us. They have lived for us.

A principle so universal must harmonize with the justice of a Universal Ruler. Divine justice cannot be ignored any more than our civil laws can be ignored. Man transgressing the laws of God must expect to be penalized, and he has nothing to bring with which to erase the penalty. Then nothing but the vicarious element remains. Either that, or man is forever lost. Either accept the cross or go down to defeat and despair.

By experience we learn to know that the vicarious element satisfies and brings peace as nothing else can. There are a few things which may assist our faith—frail and faltering as it always is: the miraculous conception; His sin-free life lived under circumstances both private and public which were not conducive to a perfect life; the celestial voices uttering their approval at His baptism and on the Mount of Transfiguration; and lastly, and chief of them all, His resurrection from the dead. That is God's final approval. So it was for Paul who said, "He was declared to be the Son of God with power by the resurrection from the dead." And if He was the Son of God He would not lie about the way and the plan executed by divine counsel.

Wonderful God and wonderful Savior manifest in such a wonderful way! Where there was no way God made one.

A Market for the Poor

Ho, every one that thirsteth, come ye to the waters, and he that hath no money; come ye, buy, and eat; yea, come, buy wine and milk without money and without price. Wherefore do ye spend money for that which is not bread? and your labour for that which satisfieth not? hearken diligently unto me, and eat ye that which is good, and let your soul delight itself in fatness.   Isaiah 55:1-2

THE prophet here dips into the New Testament Gospel ministrations and pours out the gracious love of a heavenly Father. Isaiah speaks as though he had walked with the Master and had heard Him discourse about the Kingdom of Grace. Strange indeed that he, surrounded as he was by the Law on every hand, should so discern the heart of God; that he understood the processes of salvation so clearly and envisaged a dispensation rich in grace, long years before the coming of the kingdom. The chapter is a gospel call to a fallen nation, an invitation to a degraded, thirsting race. The Evangelists who spoke for the new covenant could write no more.

The Gospel bears certain distinguishing marks, and they are the same wherever you find them. They are these: propitiation, pardon, and purity. Isaiah's concept of propitiation is clearly set forth in the Fifty-third chapter of the book which bears his name. The principle of the substitutionary sacrifice is asserted there. Pardon and purity are the gifts proclaimed in this chapter.

The Gospel—the good tidings of salvation— whether found upon the greying Old Testament scrolls or inscribed upon the New Testament records, brings a joy and a satisfaction that fills a universal need. The Gospel constitutes a poor man's market where priceless things can be purchased without money. Where money is the medium of exchange for all material transactions, it is hard to understand that spiritual things can be acquired without it. In the spiritual field, all men are poor, and only those who know privation will care to buy. They have nothing to bring, nothing wherewith to make any payment, and still the market is for them. God planned it so. "The payment has been made by the owner and all the profit accrues to the purchaser." That sounds unreasonable, as it always will, unless we learn to know something

of the great love which prompted this market: a
market where you need no money, where the
most precious things are given away. That is how
God deals with men, and that is the story which
we call the Gospel. The market is the same whether we find it in the Old or the New Testament,
because with God there is no change, not even
the "shadow of turning." Thanks be to God who
planned so well and whose plans can be trusted
not to miscarry. Our need is great—very great, and
save for the supplies graciously provided by our
Father in heaven, we would perish on the way.

The need which is ours we may not fully understand. We do know that there is within our hearts
a deep longing for something, which makes us
reach out. There is a strange emptiness within,
and we sense that something is lacking. We need
more than bread and butter to feed the body;
we need more than clothes to cover it; we need
more than a house to shelter it. Always we thirst
for something beyond our material possessions.
These are good to have, but they are not enough.
How much we are blessed, we who have an abundance of material things, we will never fully realize
until they are abruptly taken from us.

I do not believe that all men consciously thirst
after God. We know many people who seem to be
perfectly contented spiritually—who have no need
of God—who can live in a world surrounded by

the glory of God and yet never ask about Him or
seem to care whether they know Him or not. Yet
they surely thirst and reach out for something
which lies beyond. There is an instinctive urge
which keeps calling them to reach for more than
they possess. That is the thirst after God, because
God alone can satisfy it. That is why Augustine
could say, "Thou hast created us for Thyself, and
restless are our hearts within us until they repose
in Thee."

Many do not thirst after forgiveness, though
they will never really be happy and contented until they know what forgiveness means. Those
there are who are not thirsting for holiness, and
yet they will never be blessed until they are holy.
Men may not really feel any need of God, yet they
will never be satisfied until they have found Him.
Isaiah's call in this chapter is wide and clear. It is
a call to every thirsting one, every longing one,
wherever in the wide world he may be. It is the
business of the church to awaken these dormant
desires after God, after forgiveness, after holiness
—to make men need-conscious. No season in the
entire church year, rich as it is, is designed more
than Lent to both create and to satisfy man's need.

It has been said that "hunger and thirst increase
with the store." How true that is. You spent years
planning the house which you wanted as a per-
manent home. And you planned well, both for

convenience and comfort. You soon learned that some things had been omitted. Because you had a good house you wanted more. You were fortunate in your investments, the fruits of your labors were abundant, you acquired considerable wealth. Were you satisfied? You wanted more. The thirst was still there. You acquired an education because you wanted to learn to enjoy more things, but your education only intensified your desires. So it is for everyone. Nothing really satisfies, and one sometimes wonders why so many are ceaselessly bent on securing things proved by experience to be so utterly unsatisfying. Isaiah asks the question, "Why do you spend your money for that which is not bread?" Why are men "weighing out their lives, spending their energies, wasting their affections upon that which brings no lasting satisfaction to the soul"? They seek to feed their longings, but the sense of hunger remains. They fill up their lives, and still, paradoxically, they are empty. Why spend a whole life time in securing that which only makes you dissatisfied?

The world outdoing itself in excessive striving indicates how great is the thirst. Men do want to be happy and contented, and they imagine that the possession of certain things will satisfy that longing. The poor man wishes for, and works to get, more money. Maybe he should have more. But having attained his ambitions, will he be

satisfied? Ask the rich man if *he* is, as he struggles
to attain more. The ambitious man longs for fame
and honor but these do not satisfy. He must have
more to satisfy his need, and sometimes he will
stoop to unworthy means by which to attain the
worthless.

How can the longing which belongs to the soul
be satisfied through the body? It cannot be. The
longing and the thirsting cannot be satisfied by
forcing double duty upon the body. It is the soul
that is in need. "My soul is athirst after the living
God." "As the hart panteth after the water brooks,
so panteth my soul after Thee, O God." Only God
can satisfy.

The Israelites during the Babylonian captivity
sought release from their pain in the work at hand.
They were an unfortunate people. Many of them
lost all hope and all their faith in the covenant
promises. As a nation they were degraded and in
bondage. They were changed. The happy carefree
people could not sing the old songs any more, so
"they hanged their harps on a willow tree." Most
of them forgot about God. They remembered Jerusalem no more. Trade and business became a substitute for their religion. They concentrated upon
commerce and gain. "From being a nation of born
priests, they became a nation of born traders."
Gain took the place of God. The exiles amassed
money, the carnal appetites were fed. "The body

luxuriated but the soul languished." They said to their souls, "Thou hast much goods laid up, eat, drink, and be merry," but the souls cried, "We thirst." The body toiled, the mind schemed, the eyes coveted, but the soul kept on crying, "I thirst."

The disciples who had been with Jesus found that that fellowship satisfied their thirst. When He was taken from them, Peter was the first to suggest that they go back to their work.

Many a man has sought to bury himself in work, thus to stifle the cry within. But what would such a one do when the work was done? The day does come when man can work no more. How terrible the thirst would be then.

The ascetic schools and the hermits have sought to create a lasting happiness for themselves by renouncing all material things and entering voluntary privation. Imposing self-inflicted penalties will not satisfy. To mortify the body will not improve the soul.

In the hope of refreshing its weary soul, the world repairs to amusements. It is one round of pleasure, gaiety, and excitement the livelong day. While it lasts, there will be some satisfaction. But how short the time it lasts. Then the soul cries for more. I thirst, I thirst! New pleasures are sought as the old ones fail. Something new, something that thrills. Around and around it goes. They are chasing shadows, and when night falls what will the harvest be?

Thank God, man's thirst can be quenched. There is a true source of satisfaction, and those fountains flow freely. God's grace is sufficient to meet all our needs, and the living waters from the throne of God can quench our nameless thirst. Nothing the world can give is proportionate to our need, for the soul of man cannot be fed on husks.

The story is told of a shipwrecked crew that had been drifting for days, suffering the horrors of thirst. A vessel was seen approaching them just as they had abandoned all hope. When the vessel came near they cried as best they could through throats that were parched, "We are thirsty—we need water." "Dip your bucket over the side," came back the mocking answer. Unconsciously they had drifted into that part where the mighty fresh water Amazon sent her waters far out into the sea. They were floating in an ocean of plenty. Yet they knew it not. There are oceans of plenty around us, as the grace of God is poured out in abundance through the Word and in the Sacraments. Humanity is expending itself—expiring in vain efforts, while there are oceans of happiness accessible.

To a world famishing, thirsting, and dying, *that* sounds extravagant. But let God get hold of you and you will know that He can take care of all your needs.

Lent brings God very near to us; it makes Him real. For as the Son is, so is the Father. Lent reveals God's great love for us, and this love gives us an unfailing hope in Jesus Christ. Jesus came into this thirsting, famishing world, and He knew what His mission was. Jesus knew our need. The parables spoken by Him prove that. The incident with the Samaritan woman at Jacob's well in Sychar, to whom Jesus spoke about "living water," proves that He knew and understood our needs. This woman had drunk from many wells to quench her thirst, but she always thirsted again. Jesus said unto her, "He that drinketh of the water that I shall give him shall never thirst." In the sixth chapter of John, He discourses about Himself and says, "I am the bread of life . . . he that eateth of this bread shall live forever."

He takes care of all our needs. Nothing has escaped His attention, nothing is left undone. He has provided for us as only the Creator and Preserver of the universe could provide. Are you struggling under a burden of sin—are you heavy-laden with guilt? He takes care of that, for "the blood of Jesus cleanseth from all sin." How differently you will view the world and all that it holds if you know that your sins are forgiven. All things become new, then. Maybe you are the vic-

tim of some sin which has made life unbearable
for you. Remember that "He giveth power to the
faint, and to them that have no might he in-
creaseth strength .... they that wait for Jehovah
shall renew their strength." Your battle is hard,
the struggle seems futile, the law requires so much.
Then listen to Paul and his counsel: "Christ is
the end of the law for righteousness to everyone
that believeth."

"If the Son therefore shall make you free, ye
shall be free indeed"; that is what Jesus taught.
Are your temptations many? The Lord knows they
are, "For he was tempted in all things like as we
are." Why was He tempted? So that "He might be
touched with a feeling of our infirmities." "Let
us therefore come boldly unto the throne of grace,
that we may obtain mercy, and find grace to help
in time of need."

What are we asked to pay? Not a thing. Jesus
comes into the world's market place with His
pierced hands full of gifts. He only asks us to accept them. But here is the tragedy: one after another passes Him by. Men only shake their heads
at Him.

Shall we make that mistake too? Upon the high-
ways of life so many are crying their wares for
sale. What shall we do about it? By the grace of
God we shall not spend our money for that which
is not bread. But come what may, mockery, perse-

cution, death—I shall open wide my hand and my heart and receive for the asking that which I need most of all. Then all thirsts will be satisfied, for He becomes my all in all—all in life, all in death. Thanks be to God for everything.

Triumphant Warriors

Finally, my brethren, be strong in the Lord, and in the power of his might. Put on the whole armour of God, that ye may be able to stand against the wiles of the devil. For we wrestle not against flesh and blood, but against principalities, against powers, against the rulers of the darkness of this world, against spiritual wickedness in high places. Wherefore take unto you the whole armour of God, that ye may be able to withstand in the evil day, and having done all, to stand. Stand therefore, having your loins girt about with truth, and having on the breast-plate of righteousness; and your feet shod with the preparation of the gospel of peace; above all, taking the shield of faith, wherewith ye shall be able to quench all the fiery darts of the wicked. And take the helmet of salvation, and the sword of the Spirit which is the word of God: praying always with all prayer and supplication in the Spirit, and watching thereunto with all perseverance and supplication for all saints.　　　　Ephesians 6:10-18

"IS there not a warfare unto man upon earth, and are not his days like the days of a hireling?" So said Job in a pessimistic mood when life's stern reality dawned upon him. Yes, there is a spiritual conflict from which we dare not shrink. Various ascetic schools have tried to avoid this conflict, only to find that the prince of darkness pursued them even into remote and secret places. Even the wilderness could provide no shelter from the enemy. Jesus, too, felt the impact of this conflict when He prayed for His disciples, saying, "I pray not that thou shouldst take them out of the world, but that thou shouldst keep them from the evil one."

On occasions we may be permitted to rise onto the mountain top to view the scenes from a vantage point of glory—have a momentary transfiguration —only to be thrust into the valley below where the shadows lie and where the battle rages with un- abated violence. From the mountain top one can see farther, but the Lord's conquest is waged in the valley.

The conflict Job has in mind and to which Paul refers in our text is not a conflict with flesh and blood. Paul is calling for enlistments in the great spiritual army, and offering the offensive and de- fensive weapons to be employed in the contest with all the forces of evil which Satan has rallied to his support.

"For we wrestle . . . against principalities, against powers, against the rulers of the darkness of this world, against spiritual wickedness in high places." It is a struggle unto death with the enemies of our salvation. The soldier of the cross will be called upon to face human enemies. Persecution may overtake him; many of those to whom Paul had spoken and written gave their lives in the outbreaks of violence; but there is an enemy to be feared even more.

The forces of evil have fallen into acts of such unequaled violence that the experiences of this present generation will be long remembered. Perhaps the worst is yet to come. The foundation stones have long trembled while the multitudes have been crying for this orgy of licentiousness, this carnival of debauchery, this slaughter upon a hundred battlefields. The world has said long enough—and many of us listened: "Forget the antiquated commandments of God, let us eat, drink, and be merry for tomorrow we may die." "The nations rage and the peoples imagine a vain thing. The kings of the earth set themselves, and the rulers take counsel together saying: Let us break their bonds and cast away their cords from us." The world by its God-denying, God-defying arrogance, gets what it asks for. Evil is viciously apparent. In the words of the parable we can say, "An enemy hath done this." Surely, with all these experiences, we are not going to sing,

"It matters not how strait the gate,
How charged with punishment the scroll,
I am the master of my fate,
The captain of my soul."

That kind of philosophy invites trouble. I cannot depend upon my own direction and leadership. The world, because of its philosophy, is paid off in chaos and confusion. Without divine leadership, that is where we all end.

If we hope to emerge victorious in this conflict, to keep our freedoms, "we must put on the whole armor of God." There will be no military bands with martial music to create a frenzied loyalty, no applause from the galleries.

"Ours not to reason why,
Ours not to make reply,
Ours but to do and die."

God has heard the perishing cry from the multitudes that have gone down into the valley, and in His love He provides weapons of offense and defense against which the prince of darkness and his legions cannot stand. "For the weapons of our warfare are not carnal, but mighty before God to the casting down of strongholds." That is Paul's evaluation of God's abundant provision. Could we ask for more?

It is strange how totally Christocentric all of
Paul's presentations are. Everything for Christ.
And Christ for everyone.

Let us look for a few moments at this armor of
God, about which Paul is writing. "Stand therefore having your loins girded with truth." What
is this truth which we are asked to use? Jesus once
said, you will recall, "I am the truth." And the
apostle John says, "We beheld his glory as the
only begotten of the Father, full of grace and
truth." We must gird ourselves with Jesus—only
He can create and maintain that spirit of readiness
which is so essential. Only Jesus!

Paul says, too, "Put on the breastplate of righteousness." What is that breastplate which is called
righteousness? We may have to go clear back to
Jeremiah for an answer, but it is there. "Behold
the days come saith Jehovah, that I will raise unto
David a righteous branch, and he shall be king
and deal wisely—and this is his name whereby he
shall be called, the Lord our Righteousness." Only
Jesus again! No other breastplate will do. That
armor cannot be pierced.

Paul adds that we must have "the feet shod with
the preparation of the gospel of peace." Shod with
peace. We can do better when there is peace within—peace with God. The walk may be long and
hard, and we need good shoes for the march. The
prophet Isaiah, the great seer who penetrated the

mists of seven hundred years, had this to say about
the coming Messiah: "He shall be called Wonderful, Counsellor, Mighty God, Prince of Peace." On
the night in which Jesus was born the angels sang,
"Peace on earth." Again, the apostle Paul, writing
to the Ephesians about the reconciliation wrought
in Christ Jesus, says, "For he is our peace." Again
Jesus only!

"Taking up the shield of faith" is another pre-
caution we must take. Paul must have been observ-
ing the Roman soldier who guarded him. He does
not forget any part of the armor. Here it is the
shield that must be employed. It will be needed
often in the conflict. John says, "This is the victory
which overcometh the world, even our faith." Jesus says, "Be of good cheer for I have overcome
the world." The author of the Book of Hebrews
calls Jesus, "the author and finisher of our faith."
Jesus only! He is our all in all.

"And take the helmet of salvation." Even the
Psalmist could sing of salvation, and he said, "The
Lord is my light and my salvation." Simeon, hold-
ing the Christ-child in his arms, could say, "Now
lettest thou thy servant depart in peace—for mine
eyes have seen thy salvation." Jesus only!

Jesus is our *truth,* our *righteousness,* our *peace,*
our *faith* and our *salvation.* He is the armor God
has provided, and He is an armor in which we
shall be able "to withstand in the evil day." This

armor may be marked by many battles, but it
grows stronger with the years.

The Lord has not only planned that we should
resist evil at every turn of the way. We are told
to *overcome* it. For this purpose He has provided
offensive weapons. Be ready to attack.

"Take the sword of the Spirit which is the Word
of God." In his incomparable Gospel, John begins
by calling Jesus the Word. "In the beginning was
the Word." And in the Apocalypse John says, "I
saw the heavens opened and behold a white horse,
and he that sat upon him was called Faithful and
True—and he was arrayed in a garment dipped in
blood, and his name is called The Word of God."
In His name shall the kingdoms of evil be at-
tacked, and in His name shall the powers of evil
be routed. Jesus only.

Then, we must not neglect "praying at all sea-
sons in the Spirit." When we struggle with the
enemy, when we are surrounded by temptations,
sin, and death, then the day of trouble has come.
When I cry unto the Lord for deliverance I dare
approach only in the merits of Him who died for
me. It may be a call out of the depths, but out of
the depths He will hear me, for the name of Jesus
made a way where there was no way. Jesus is my
prayer and in His name I shall go from strength
to strength, from victory to victory. No name but
the name of Jesus will do.

In short, to put on the armor of God is to put on Christ Jesus. "If any man be in Christ Jesus, he is a new creature." He who has put on the whole armor of God, "is strong in the might of the Lord." The pathway of the Christian may not be easy, but it is victorious. For the might of the Lord is "far above all principality and power and might and dominion, and every name that is named, not only in this world but in that also which is to come." If I trust in Him who guides the destiny of every star, who rules the universe so well, I "shall not be put to shame."

When the ancient Hebrews drew out their armies and went to war against their enemies and the time of battle was at hand, the high priest presented himself at the head of the army and spoke these words to them, "Be not in fear of your enemies for the Lord your God fights for you."

Oh, how we need men and women who will not be afraid! Men and women who will not be led astray by subtle fads and spiritual innovations. Men and women who will not be ashamed to own His cause or blush to speak His name. Men and women who will stand alone if need be, like the soldier of Pompeian tradition who died sword in hand.

Trying times will come. Times when, with Jeremiah, we will cry, "O that I had in the wilderness a lodging place for wayfaring men." The days may be hard, days when we will cry with the "saints their watches keeping, How long?"

Out of Roman tradition an interesting legend comes to us. Peter, visiting the Roman congregation during the fierce Neronic persecutions, was finally persuaded by the members that he must not remain in the city. He questioned the voice that urged him to go, but finally he yielded and went out upon the Appian way where he met Christ. A poet has written what is supposed to have transpired on the way in these words:

O king of David's lineage
Whither goest, Peter wondering cried.
To Rome, the Master said,
To be crucified.
Into the night the vision ebbed like breath,
And Peter turned and rushed on Rome and death.

Our part in this great conflict may be very small, indeed, but it will constitute a real part. We may be only a wheel in the mechanism of God's universe, but we may be very essential.

It is better to be in the struggle with Christ than to be in peace where He is not.

What Will the
Harvest Be?

*For the wages of sin is death; but the gift of God is
eternal life through Jesus Christ our Lord.* Romans 6:23

THE dark and brutal events related to the passion of our Lord reveal the vicious qualities of
sin. The implications of sin are many, and they
are serious. The problems imposed by sin are not
remote, for they touch the lives of everyone. The
business man who employs labor must reckon with
sin; the banker in selecting his aides is confronted
by the same problem; the individual or the group
who seeks to provide amusements and relaxation
for our tired American people knows how sin
enters everywhere and must be reckoned with in
all its multiple forms. The church, the home, the

school—all these know the problems posed by evil
and the devastating effects of all forms of sin upon
the social structure. Sin dogs the professional man,
hounds the business man, and haunts the spirit of
the man who labors. It meets you in the home, on
the busy thoroughfares, and even in the sanctuaries of God. Everywhere the ugly face of sin leers.

The problem of sin is, of all problems, the most
personal and the most sordidly practical. You cannot escape its force. Sin filters into all our relationships — social, industrial, and political. It even
taints our religious aspirations. Every vexing situa-
tion that arises is prompted by some sin, some-
where. The pressure may be exerted from within
or without. An error that is universal is funda-
mental. Get rid of sin and most of the evils we
know will be eliminated.

The State recognizes sin as a ravaging curse
which it cannot escape. It may be called by a different name, but it still remains sin. Legislation
has been given a thoroughgoing test in its ability
to hold evil in check. The results are disappoint-
ing. Education has been tried with equally dis-
couraging results. You can not legislate your way
into righteousness, nor can you, by the reading of
books, find your way out of evil. An error as fun-
damental as sin can only be mastered from the
inside. The heart that is cleansed and renewed is
really prepared for the conflict. By the grace of

God that consummation may be realized. The corrective lies with the individual.

The fatality of sin is indelibly inscribed upon all historic records. Sin means death to the individual, death to the commonwealth, death to the nation, death to all that is good and noble. It eventuates always in death.

Sometimes we call sin a transgression. It simply means going over a line where one has no right to go. Have you, in your conduct, ever gone over that line? Often. Sometimes we call sin iniquity. It is an inequity. Are there no inequities in your life—no deviations from the right? Sometimes we speak of sin as guile and treachery. Sometimes we call it lawlessness. That is a good definition, because all true law is an expression of God's will, and resistance to that will is lawlessness or rebellion. Sin is an act of the will. It sets itself to resist God.

Surely sin is a disease, a debt, a load, a galling, intolerable slavery. "The way of the transgressor is hard." A man ought to get rid of it, though it should require the severing of a hand or the plucking of an eye. Jesus knew the awful power and tyranny of sin in the Garden of Gethsemane when "His sweat was as it were great drops of blood." He knew the awful consequences of sin when He struggled alone on the cross as our Substitute and when His lacerated spirit cried, "My God, My

God, why hast thou forsaken me?" That is the price the sinner pays.

"The wages of sin is death." Sin employs labor and pays wages. Everyone who works for sin gets his wages. You may be willing to forgive the account, but sin insists on paying. Sin insists on accuracy, and to be sure that those standards are maintained, usually pays in kind. For each of my transgressions, sin gives me a definite and exact equivalent. I may squander my substance in riotous living, and I reap privation; I may neglect or abuse my health, and my body breaks; I may deceive another, and he will deceive me; I may curse another, and he will curse me; I may turn my back upon the crucified Savior, and He will eventually turn away from me. "It is a very prosaic truth that the payment made to the sinner is of the same stuff as sin." Sin in the realm of the body brings its result in the body. Sin in the realm of mind brings a degenerating recompense. Sin against the soul brings death to it. Jacob deceived his own blind father, and his sons deceived him. He wronged his brother Esau, and his favorite son, Joseph, was wronged by his brothers. He used a kid in his scheme to deceive his father, and years later his sons used the blood of a kid to give color to the mantle of Joseph.

With bitter tenacity of memory David learned that sin pays in kind. It infected his own house and spread contagion through the whole kingdom.

Sin does not pay all the wages at once. The logical and summary result will be death. Payments are made on sort of an installment plan. They have only been precursors, fragments of the whole wage which is death. You have received your earnest money, but when life's day is over the whole payment will be forthcoming. It pays here and now in disorder, loss, calamity, disease, sorrow, discontent, hatred, treachery, remorse, and achings of the soul. If the secret of every heart were known, the world would not find tears enough to shed over the terrible devastation.

"The wages of sin is death." The woes endured here are merely a prelude to that which is to be. Sin and death are only different phases of the same thing. Sin is death begun. Death is the final stage of sin.

In our Swinton's Fifth Reader, almost fifty years ago, there appeared a little tragic story that I have long remembered. It is a story about the quicksands on the beaches of Brittany, a province jutting into the sea on the west coast of France. A man is walking there enjoying the afternoon sun and the fresh ocean breezes. He is not aware that the ground underneath him is soft and that his feet are beginning to sink deeper and deeper. He is lost in his reveries, elated by the new experience of walking on the shores of Brittany, and he never senses the danger. He begins to feel that the walking is heavy; his feet are cumbersome. Strange, he thinks. Then, all of a sudden, it flashes upon his mind that the tide is out and the beds of quicksand have been exposed. He tries to move more quickly. His feet sink deeper. He begins to plunge madly, calling for help. There is no one to hear. He sinks deeper and deeper into the smooth, slippery sand. It reaches His knees, his loins, and his waist. He stretches out his hands, piteously calling for help. The tremendous pressure causes him to bleed at the nose, and soon only his head remains above the ground. Then only a smooth stretch of shining sand remains. The sky is blue, the sun is shining, and the waves of the sea gently wash and lap as the tide returns. The man is gone.

The law of gravitation is merciless and inexorable. The same action marks the law of sin. It is merciless and it is inexorable. Death is the end.

Is there no help? Is there not someone who can hear our call and who has the will and the power to lift us out of the quagmire of sin? There *is* One who has come to us out of another sphere, "one who was tried in all things like as we are." He had no sin, yet "the blood of Jesus Christ cleanseth us from all sin." "He who knew no sin was made to be sin for us." Death was set to swallow us up, and He met death at Calvary; and He vanquished the monster. Death itself was swallowed up in victory.

He offers His victory over sin and death as a free gift to us. He pays no wages, but He grants us life and salvation as a gift of His grace.

How hard the struggle—how sweet the peace He gives.

That is the Gospel truth—it is Good News for every sinner.